MY ONE
GOOD NERVE

MY ONE GOOD NERVE

Ruby Dee

To Roxanne —
Glorious Life!
Ruby Dee
8/14/99

John Wiley & Sons, Inc.
New York • Chichester • Weinheim • Brisbane • Singapore • Toronto

Copyright © 1987 and 1999 by Ruby Dee. All rights reserved.
Published by John Wiley & Sons, Inc.
Published simultaneously in Canada

"Today Is Ours Let's Live It" from *Freedomways Magazine* Vol. 4, No. 1, 1964. Author unknown.

Photo credits: p. 30, Friedman-Abeles; p. 52, Columbia Pictures Corp.; p. 70 & p. 92, Chris Bennion; p. 148, Gereghty, Columbia Pictures Corp.; p. 166, Anthony Barboza

Good faith efforts have been made to trace and obtain permission from the copyright holders of the photographs and excerpts included in this book. In the event we have overlooked a necessary permission, please contact the publisher so that we may make appropriate arrangements.

Library of Congress Cataloging-in-Publication Data:
Dee, Ruby.
    My one good nerve / Ruby Dee.
        p.   cm.
    ISBN 0-471-31704-7 (alk. paper)
    1. Afro-Americans—Literary collections.   I. Title.
    PS3554.E3432M9   1998
    818'.5409—dc21   98-25196

Printed in the United States of America

10 9 8 7 6 5 4 3 2 1

To Daddy and Mother,
Ed and Em.

Contents

Today Is Ours

Preface

I believe we are made up of all we absorb, which makes finding a distinct personality a serious challenge. I've sensed and been told that as an actor I'm not easy to define. But who is? I consider a certain flexibility, a chameleonlike adaptability, a positive attribute.

Like anyone who is still testing the depth and temperature of personal waters, I am indebted to many people. I am inspired by Zora Neale Hurston, Gwendolyn Brooks, Sonia Sanchez, Carolyn Rodgers, Paule Marshall, Alice Walker, Toni Morrison, Toni Cade Bambara, Lindamichelle Baron, and Rosa Guy—to name just a very few women whose writing has encouraged me to walk on out. What they write has assured me that the waters will hold or will part for safe passage to surer shores.

Walking ideas and words is what I'm mostly about. "What words and ideas?" you might wonder. As I tell the audiences for my one-woman show, *My One Good Nerve,* "Welcome to my house of words . . . words that laugh, words that weep, words that shout, and words so deep and so private they refuse to give their names even to their lover. . . ."

Several years ago, with encouragement from Ossie Davis, my husband, enthusiastic listeners, other writers, and friends, I decided to publish some of the pieces that I had written and performed on campuses, in theaters, on television, at benefits, for funerals, and just for fun. Chicago publisher and poet Haki Madhubuti stopped the messing around and put the book in print. Now I've added some new pieces, changed the collection, and taken the words on a second go 'round.

As time passes, some things do not change, of course. I remain as grateful as ever: To John Henrik Clarke, who arranged my first book assignment, *Glowchild,* a collection of poetry mostly written by young people; to James L. Hicks who firmly nudged me into writing a weekly column for the *New York Amsterdam News*; to Ruth Gordon, the actor, whose almost first words to me years ago were, "You must write!"; to Kathleen Karter, Lynne Palmer, and Kathy Collins, tenders of mind and soul shops; to my children Nora, Guy, and Hasna. Nora critiqued and discussed and deleted some of the bawdiness. ("We don't want to get banned anywhere as with

Glowchild.") Hasna wrote the poem "I Just Couldn't," but she insisted that she didn't want to take credit as an author because she had written it so long ago and I had changed too much of it for her to claim. "No, I'm giving it to you, Mom. Don't put my name on it," she said. I said okay, but sometimes moms lie.

I add my deep thanks to Carole Hall, at John Wiley & Sons, for deciding to publish this book, selecting the material, arranging the sections, and suggesting that I write the section introductions. Cheers to Latifah Salahuddin for her quiet patience and efficiency and to my incredible husband, Ossie.

Finally, dear readers, I am appreciative of your company in sharing these words. There are words beyond words that only the open and understanding heart can decipher. For your welcome in opening this book, I feel a gratitude that words cannot express.

Introduction

The author of this book is not the same absolutely pure and sweet woman who was Nat King Cole's girlfriend in the film *The Saint Louis Blues,* or the fresh-faced bride of Jackie Robinson in *The Jackie Robinson Story,* or the long-suffering wife of Sidney Poitier in *A Raisin in the Sun.* Part of her, yes, is those women, but only part. Most women, I imagine—and surely Ruby—are a complex of many women. Few, perhaps, have remained as well hidden by only one facet of their personalities as has Ruby, the actor. Here is a Ruby Dee you may never have suspected—the writer.

Ruby, as a writer, is unique—one of a kind—which means she can only be compared with herself. Nothing about her work reminds me of anybody; all of it stands alone.

This does not mean that what she writes is esoteric, or exclusive, or private. Her meaning, her rhythm, and her insights are not mysterious, or enigmatic. What she has to say is wide open, free, immediately available to the curious. She has no puzzles that she dares the reader to solve. What she has to say is always public and will fit into any imagination—but only on Ruby's terms.

She tears the world apart as a child might do, and then, right before your eyes, she builds it back together again. The same old world, but through Ruby's eyes—it looks brand-new.

There is a profound simplicity in this point of view most times, which to appreciate requires that I become profoundly simple in my own point of view. Reading Ruby can be disarming.

Most of us grow up as quickly as we have to, getting further away by the day from who we were when we were children. We shorten our sails, temper our ambitions, and set aside our fondest expectations in order to face the day. But Ruby reminds us that a simpler world is only a thought away, with the light still glowing in undiminished vigor right in the middle of our secret mind. All we have to do is open our eyes, turn the page, and read.

—Ossie Davis

Sounds in the
Darkness

Lots of people, including myself, are longing for impossibilities.

I write about the things my baby sister LaVerne and I used to reminisce about together as a way of keeping her close to me. I used to do all her fight-ing for her. She brought out the protector in me. She knew she could always count on me to be there for her at crunch time, and I was, too. Except for the last time I heard her call my name. I heard it coming all the way from Las Vegas to Los Angeles, but at the time I didn't believe calls for help could come through the air and not on the telephone. Besides, I knew I would be going to Vegas in another ten days. I let that word, "tomorrow," and thoughts of "later" beckon me instead. Ten days later she had died, and I didn't get to embrace her or say good-bye when I could have.

I used to tease LaVerne about how much more of our childhood she remembered than I did. The South. Harlem. Of course, I remember some things perfectly, like one particular woman, a retired teacher, who used to visit our mother. Even her laughter seemed sad. My mother rented rooms in our spacious apartment up on Sugar Hill, mostly to domestics. They lived with us a long time and only came home on Thursdays, every other Sunday, and on their one week vacation during the year.

Life exacts a high toll, sometimes all at once, and sometimes bit by bit.

Remembrance

I have a younger sister who remembers everything. I believe she even remembers being born—what it was like inside and so forth.

Her memories have helped to inform me of who I am and why I feel the way I do about certain things. Take poverty, for example. She said that when I was a baby I was put to bed in a dresser drawer because the folks who kept me during a parental shift of emphasis were very poor and couldn't afford a crib. So, poverty came to mean a gasping for breath in darkness, a claustrophobic condition where you could smother to death unless you were big enough and strong enough to kick the drawers open.

Every summer, my mother used to take us to Chester, South Carolina, to visit her people. I have some of my own memories about that time. The South came to mean thick milk, bitter greens, great big ol' biscuits, and oh such sweet peaches, flies, heat, quilting with my grandma, hugging my bearded grandfather who smelled of tobacco and horses and sweat. It was a good smell.

Back then, I thought there was no such thing as ugly white people and I thought all mean people looked like conductors. My sister says I once kicked a conductor who got our mother upset and threatened to put us off the train when she couldn't find the pass we traveled on. I thought the boogeyman wore white sheets and all colored people were good and sang spirituals. And when something bad happened, they grunted and said, "Humph! Ah Lord!" And when they died they got hung on trees.

My sister asks sometimes, "Remember those horsehair mattresses we slept on and how we'd bury our faces in the pillows because that coarse linen smelled so fresh?" I really do remember the sound of the screen door banging and all the bustling around and excitement when it came time for us to leave and looking forward to the heavy lunch Grandma had packed for us to eat on the train. Then there were my cousins, Sipp and Jay. Sipp's name was really Esther. But big Jay would always be clowning around. He used to make us pretty rings out of peach pits. He'd put a bead in the middle of it and he'd say, "See that. That's a diamond. Don't tell nobody I never gave you nothing." He had one joke he'd tell. I don't remember what it was but the punchline was, "Niggers just ain't no good."

One time, my brother Edward showed him his medals that he'd won in school for running and jumping and Jay said, "I bet you stole 'em. I bet the only medals you ever won were for running to the table and jumping in the bed."

And when it came time for us to get on the wagon and head out for the train depot, he and Edward would chuck rocks at each other until somebody would tell them to stop.

South was where almost everybody we knew came from. South was where you went to visit in the summertime or brought people away from who were in trouble. When somebody died, you took the body back home, down South. South was where my mother had taught school. South was where colored people had a lot of land that peanuts and cotton sucked dry. They couldn't hold on to it, so they just walked off and left it; or there was land where the old folks got killed and somebody took it. South was where chickens came from and where you could see pigs and ride horses, milk cows. Later South was stories about swamps and snakes and alligators and walking in ditches so white folks could pass, and South was about running away. It was Billie Holiday singing, "Southern trees bear a strange fruit." South was where that same cousin Jay came back home from the war, sat on the edge of his bed in his uniform, put a pistol in his mouth and blew his brains out. "Humph! Ah Lord!"

South was a scary place where skeletons and ghosts cracked pecans in the night. It was a warm, loving/hating, sensuous, personal, personal place. Whenever I hear somebody say, "I'm from the South," it sounds like a confession.

Oh yes, my sister remembers a lot and she helps me remember some things too. I told her she's the one in the family that ought to be a writer. I believe she could fill a book from just memories.

Three Finger Freddie

Being black in the U.S. of A. can be especially hard on some people. Three Finger Peg Leg One Eye Hook Freddie was one of those people. As you may guess from his accumulation of names, the vicissitudes of blackness had chopped him up pretty bad. None of his friends and few of his family ever thought he'd live long. I know I didn't, but he is still hanging in there.

My name is Axel, the closest thing to Freddie's best friend, you might say. Perhaps one reason we got so close is—well, I'm an insignificant-looking person, and Freddie is so big and black and important looking. Opposites attracting and all that. Now Freddie never would have been good-looking, but his present condition made him look downright scary and hard for somebody to think about hiring. But I'm getting ahead of myself.

You see, he got the name of Three Finger when he was still a boy. One day after regular school hours, he was experimenting around in the chemistry room when the custodian opened the door and startled him by yelling, "What the hell you doing in there, nigger?"

Freddie dropped the concoction he'd been working on, which exploded and blew off two of his fingers. On top of that, he hurt his head as he fell to the floor. He remained in a coma for two days. When he came to, the first thing he said was, "I am not a nigger. I ain't a nigger. I ain't."

Then he told his momma and me what happened. Now we believe that it was being called a nigger like that, that was at the root of the robbery of Freddie bit by bit and brought on his present predicament. The word became like a red flag to a bull. He just naturally went crazy anytime somebody called him a nigger—especially somebody white. It stands to reason that that kind of sensitivity can be costly. Even though, over the years, Freddie inflicted a lot of punishment on a lot of people, he himself suffered the loss of some pretty important parts.

Alright. The two fingers he lost were on the left hand. Then he lost all of his right hand in an ax fight he had with a guard on the chain gang. I never did get all the details on the stick fight he had with some bruiser in Louisiana where he lost his left eye. He lost a leg when a bus got in his way as he was crossing the road to deal with another white "brother" who had said, "Come on over here a minute, nigger, please. I got something I want you to help me with."

His momma and I had warned him over and over: "You can not let ignorant people rile you up like this. You can't keep a-gettin' mad every time some fool—no matter what they color—gets it in his head to call you a nigger. Keep on like this and you will lose your behind."

I said, "Define *yourself.* You know who you are."

"He's not been himself since that explosion in high school," his momma said.

"I am not a nigger. I ain't a nigger. I ain't," the by now Three Finger Peg Leg, etc., Freddie would protest over and over, sitting with his face in some corner whenever his spirits got real low.

Now, it's not so easy for a grown black man to get a job even when he has all his parts and all his faculties. An off-and-on twenty-year prison record doesn't help much either. So, naturally, after his momma passed, the question of where he was gonna get the money to survive began to worry him. Even before the loss of his various parts, he had been particular about what kind of work he wanted to do. For example, he didn't want to be a bouncer.

"Just because I'm big and black and strong, I don't want to get paid for knocking people around," he said.

But the circumstances of how life had . . . inter-coursed him up, mitigated against his having many choices.

Fortune had been kinder to me, however, who learned early, thank God, how to put the fact of my blackness in a more realistic, business perspective. I now owned a combination restaurant-club in a good location. Every now and then, Freddie would come by, before things got underway in the evening, and sit down and play a game of checkers with himself, using his three fingers to move the red checkers and the hook he had for a right hand to move the black.

The place was filling up pretty good this partic-ular night and I really wanted Freddie to go home. But he kept steady pushing those checkers and ar-guing with himself from time to time, "I am not a nigger. I ain't a *nigger*. I ain't."

The combo that entertained starting with the cocktail hour took a break, and I saw Freddie slowly get up. I thought he was fixing to leave or going over to talk to the musicians, so I wasn't prepared for what happened. Freddie hop-walked over to the little stage and sat down at the piano. With the three fingers, he began to play a rhythm in the bass that made everybody in the place turn around. Then he'd slide that hook, or hop it, all over the treble while he beat out another rhythm on the floor with the peg. After a while, it seemed that the hook got caught in some high notes and a sound came out like a wail. It reminded me of Coltrane, the way he could hammer a phrase that conjured up colors and gave vibrations concrete form in midair. The customers stopped eating, drinking, and talking and just listened. Then, all of a sudden, they stood up and shouted and clapped. I even saw some of them crying. From time to time, Freddie would grunt and mumble under his breath. I knew what he was saying.

Later that night, Freddie started in again and the people got up and danced like they were under a spell and there was no tomorrow. I wondered if they'd ever be going home. I don't know where Freddie learned to play piano like that. Maybe he picked it up in the pen. Sounds crazy to me, but he says it has a lot to do with remembering sounds and how they feel. Playing checkers helps too, he told me. Now you figure that one.

Since that night, nine years ago now, I've opened two more clubs. He works all three places, and we call them "Three Finger Freddie's" since Freddie and I are partners now. The man is hard on pianos, though, and I have had to put special wood on the floors to keep Freddie from pushing them in with that peg.

He stopped mumbling to himself about five years ago. I do notice, though, that sometimes his good eye fills up and spills over whenever he's playing something quiet and sweet. Looks like he's gotten over that word "nigger," too, because no more parts are missing that I know of. No more parts, that is, since the brawl about five years ago when he got both his eardrums broke and lost his power to hear.

While Waiting

"Someday he'll come along—that man I love,
And he'll be big and strong—"
I need to hear
Songs that I can sing
Words I can remember
Melodies that haunt
Sounds that sustain me
While waiting for that man I love
(Who I haven't even met yet)
To come get me on his fine black steed
And take me away
Gently intent on the passion
With love deed
Or he can just drive on up in his raggedy old car
Or come walkin'
I'll have his supper ready and
Leave the door ajar.
Because the wind is howling, honey,
And the coal is low.
But he better hurry up and get here
'Cause I ain't gonna wait forever.
"Someday he'll come along. That man I love—"

Aunt Zurletha

Aunt Zurletha had pretty red hair, light brown eyes, and blue-black skin. A circle of rouge was on each cheek. The shiny red lipstick on her full mouth matched her fingernail polish which matched her toenail polish. Usually, she wore earrings that looked like diamonds that matched the three rings she always wore.

My brother William said she looked like a witch, which made me wonder when and where he had ever seen a witch. My other brother, Curtis, said she looked pathetic. "Pathetic" was his new word that year. Everything was "pathetic." My father, Hosea, said she looked like a hustler. "Zurletha the Zero," he used to say. I thought she was pretty, especially when she smiled. Her teeth were even, and so white.

Mama used to say, "You can just quit so much talk about Zurletha. She's the only roomer that pays her rent in advance."

I heard her say to Hosea one night, "Who could we turn to when we had that fire in the shop and folks suing you for their clothes and the insurance company practically blaming you for starting your own fire and all the fires in Harlem for the last ten years? Who in this world could we turn to? Tell me. We would have starved to death but for Zurletha. No, I will not let you put her out."

"Now hold on, Mat. Gratitude is a thing you have got to understand. I am grateful—grateful to God who made it possible for me not to go under. That woman was just God's instrument, God's way of showing me—"

"You just mad because you can't get her to that church of yours."

"Mat, the woman needs a church home. She needs something more in her life besides those white folks she works for. She needs to find God."

"Not in that raggedy little broken-down store-front, Hosea. You know how she likes pretty things."

"That is precisely what worries me, Mat. That is precisely why I want her out of here. Take Baby—she practically worships her. And if I catch her one more time messing around in that woman's room—"

"Zurletha doesn't mind. She told me Baby's just having a little fun," Mama said.

"A little fun can leave you dragging a lifetime load. I've seen too much, Mat. I know what I'm talking about."

"Alright, Hosea—that's how you feel, we can keep Baby out of there."

"Playing with them beads and that glass junk she calls jewelry. Rubbing up against those rabbits she's got hanging on the door—"

"They are not rabbits, and you know it. Mink, that's what it is. A mink coat, and she's also got a fox stole."

"Don't care if it's dog. I want Baby's mind steady on her books and her grades and on what she is going to do with her life."

"Alright, alright, Hosea. Stop preaching at me. Put that light out now. Go on to sleep."

"Keep that door locked when Zurletha's not in there, y'hear."

I didn't understand my father sometimes. Aunt Zurletha—and he made us call her "Aunt"—had been living with us on her days off for as long as I can remember. She didn't want us to call her Miss Battles. And Hosea wouldn't let us say just "Zurletha." The people she worked for called her "Zurlie." I think that's the only thing she didn't like— "Zurlie" this and "Zurlie" that for forty years.

She was always giving us something. Gave Curtis his own radio. Gave William a microscope. My last birthday, last August, she gave me a guitar. You should've heard her play the guitar. We'd come home from Sunday school and hear her singing and stomping her foot. Made us want to dance. If Hosea came home to eat before going back to church, she'd stop. Soon as he left, though, she'd open her door, and we'd all go in, me first.

She had so many beautiful things. Real crystal glasses that she could tap with her fingernail and make sounds like music. There wasn't too much room to walk, so mostly I sat on her big brass bed. And she'd let me play with the silver candlesticks or try on the jewelry and hats. She had such pretty suitcases, too. Since the guitar, though, whenever she came home, she'd show me how to play different chords. We'd practice very quietly.

One time she took us to the beach on the subway. Hosea was in Washington, and Mama had promised us we could go. It was still dark when I heard her in the kitchen. I got up and she let me help her pack this big straw basket with all kinds of food she had brought with her the night before. William and Curtis carried the blankets. She carried the basket. I had Curtis's radio. It was a beautiful day, and we had such a good time, too, even Curtis with his smart-alecky self.

Aunt Zurletha had on a silky blue-and-green bathing suit and some kind of rubber sandals that had lots of straps and curved heels with big holes through them and her pretty red hair was tied in a ponytail and, as always, she had on her jewelry.

William and Curtis were whispering behind her back and making fun, saying she looked like a cow-pig. I think she must have heard them talking about her bunion sticking out of her strappy sandals, even though she was laughing and shaking her shoulders to the music on Curtis's radio as she set up the umbrella and opened the blankets. Later, when me and Curtis and William came out of the water, she had the lunch all set out and was stretched out reading *True Love* magazine. The sun was bouncing off her bracelet as I reached over and started twisting it around her arm. She took it off and said, "Here, you can wear it for a while." I put it on my arm and ran out from under the umbrella and started pretending I was a rich lady. William said, "You think you something, huh? She probably stole it." This time I know she heard because just before we started to eat, she took the bracelet off my arm.

"You always have such pretty things, Aunt Zurletha," I said.

And she said, "Ought to. I've been working mighty hard for a lotta years. Then, too, my people buy me—or give me—a lot of stuff. Especially when the children were small. We traveled all over then."

"They must be some rich people, man," Curtis said.

"Rich? They got money's mama," Aunt Zurletha said.

"What does money's mama look like, and who's the daddy?" William asked.

Zurletha laughed and took a dainty little bite of one of the sandwiches.

"They probably stole all that money," William said. "Hosea says that rich folks are thieves."

"Not my people," said Zurletha. "My people are just plain smart. And white, too, you know?"

I thought William sounded jealous, and mean, too.

"And how come they didn't give you some of that money instead of all that other junk?"

Aunt Zurletha didn't even seem mad.

"It's not junk, William. They give me expensive things. Years ago, too, when I wanted to bake pies to sell, they were going to set me up a place."

"What happened, Aunt Zurletha?" I asked.

Then she told us how her lady got pregnant again and didn't want her to leave, and how they kept promising to set up the pie place but never did, what with all the traveling and more babies coming; then, being in charge of opening all the different houses; and with her people getting sick and dying one right after the other; and how the children not wanting her to leave, she just finally got out of the notion of a pie place.

"Why you never got married, Aunt Zurletha?" Curtis asked.

"One time I was gonna get married—this was before you children were even thought of. But again, something came up with my people, and we stayed in Europe. I should say we stayed all over Europe for a year. And when I came back, lo and behold, he had married somebody else. Never will forget. Said it came to him that I was already married—married to a damn job, was the way he put it."

Sometimes I could just ball up my fist and hit William in the mouth.

"O-o-o, you should have quit that job, Aunt Zurletha, and married what's-his-name."

"Frank. His name was Frank." Aunt Zurletha looked sad for a second. Then she leaned over and started cutting the cake. "Then I wouldn't have you for my kids," she said.

Curtis nudged William and pointed at the kinky gray hair sticking out from under the red wig. Aunt Zurletha must have eyes all around her head, just like Mama. She fixed the wig, so the gray didn't show. And I thought it was strange—just at that moment that song "Darling I Am Growing

Old" came on the radio. Then Aunt Zurletha started singing, and doing a little dance on her tiptoes, as she passed out the cake.

I wish I could remember more about Aunt Zurletha, but she was never really home that much. I think often about her last summer with us, though. Our for-real aunt, Marie, was a nurse, and she had arranged for us to go to a summer camp for two weeks. Hosea and Mama just had to get our clothes ready—that's all. We didn't even think about Aunt Zurletha, we were having such a good time. And Mama and Hosea didn't tell us in their letter that she had been in the hospital. We didn't find out until they picked us up at the bus terminal on the way home. I was so ashamed that we hadn't thought about her. I could have drawn her a funny get-well card.

After camp, first thing, I knocked on her door and went in before she said come in. All her beautiful stuff was packed in boxes and piled on top of the radiator, and beside the window, under the bed—everywhere. It looked like she was planning to move. Everything looked gray, except for the afternoon sun against the window shade. A sweet-smelling spray mingled with the odor of—something like when Hosea found a dead mouse that had gotten caught in the little space between the stove and the sink.

I had never seen Aunt Zurletha without the wig and without the red lipstick and the beautiful earrings. Her black, black face was lying on the white, white pillow. It looked smooth like wax. Her hair was cornrowed, ending in two thin braids, and almost gone in the front and on the sides where the wig use to be. It seemed like she stayed that way for the rest of the summer.

She didn't want us children to come into her room, so I would sit on the little rug outside her door and play some of the things she had showed me on the guitar. Mama would bring food. Hosea used to say, "It's a shame. Why didn't she tell some-body she was so sick?"

Mama said, "Guess she didn't want to worry us. She complained one or two times, but she told me she just didn't have the time to go sit in some doc-tor's office."

That fall, they took her away to the hospital again. And one day while I was in school, Aunt Zur-letha died. When I came home, the room was empty. All the boxes, the brass bed, the furs, the lamps, and the glasses, the china ornaments—everything, gone.

"It just so happened, Baby," Mama said, "the people she sold all her things to came today to pick them up."

A bottle of fingernail polish was on the windowsill. It was hard to open. I don't know why, but I started painting my thumbnail. Then I found myself kneeling on the floor, with my head on the windowsill, crying. Crying like I couldn't stop. And the polish spilled all over my middy blouse. Luckily I didn't spill it all. There was a little left, and I promised myself not to ever use it, because it was all I had to remember Aunt Zurletha by.

"Nail polish? That's not what she left you, Baby," Mama said. "She left us all her cash money. She left a will. Enough for each of you to go one year in college."

"I'm hoping they will get scholarships," Hosea said.

"Well, we can see to that when the time comes." Mama started crying.

"Aw, come on now, Mat, sweetheart," Hosea said. "You know Zurletha wanted to go. See how she planned everything. Too bad, though, she never planned to get with God."

What Hosea said made me scream at him, "Yeah, but she will. And when she does, I hope she'll have on her red wig, and her rouge, and her fingernail polish, with toes to match and all her jewelry, and kiss God with her greasy lipstick on. I bet He'll just hug and kiss her back, and tell her how beautiful she is."

Daddy just looked at me a long time after that. Then he walked across the room and put his arms around me. I couldn't remember the last time he did that. He said, "Come on now. Crying won't bring her back, Baby. If crying would bring her back, maybe I'd cry along with you. Won't find another roomer who—" He went over to Mama, took her by the shoulders, and shook her a little bit before he hugged her and said, "She got to be part of this family, Mat. She really did. We're going to miss her alright. All of us."

That day I felt something that I'd been afraid of all my life tumble down inside my father and he became a gentler man. And from that day, whenever I think about Aunt Zurletha, I hear the music of crystal glasses as they touch tingling around me and I feel happy.

Bag Lady

She of middle years who
Hard-hurdled handicaps who
Had attained who
Selected from choice
Solicitations who
Flicked specks from
Pearled precise black with
Laquered nails
Was seen to
Shoulder hoist
Huge crate of
Worldly treasures
Stumble, reel, abandon
Then naked
Move on out
Into the
Thrashing sea.

Let's Talk
about Love

Let's talk about love
Because when we lack it
We rattle and bang and
Make a whole lot of racket

Love took me by complete surprise. I got a chance
to look at Mr. Ossie Davis for the first time during
a rehearsal for the Broadway show, *Jeb.* I started out
as an understudy for the role of Libby, Ossie's love
interest. William Marshall, the understudy for
Ossie, was a tall, regal-looking actor who had quite
a sense of humor. We decided that Ossie was a sur-
prisingly good actor, even though he looked like a
country bumpkin—innocent, good-natured, not-
too-bright, probably fresh from following a plow
in a cotton patch. He probably bought his clothes
secondhand with his eyes shut, we concluded
gleefully.

A week or so later, something very unsettling
occurred as Bill and I sat watching the rehearsal.
Ossie stood up on stage and silently, slowly began
tying his tie. I distinctly remember feeling something like a bolt of lightning, an electrical charge,
flash between us. It was a marvelous sensation.

31

Ossie later told me he hadn't felt a thing. Ech!
I married him anyway.

To receive love—a gift, a pat on the back, God's
grace—is difficult for some people. Embarrass-
ment, impatience, feelings of unworthiness can
get all mixed up and overshadow the fact that
divine mandates are generally executed by people.
To become an instrument of someone else's blessing
should make us feel good inside, satisfied and
happy.

Other people's happiness is intrinsic to our own.
Other people's fulfillments enhance our own and
bring us closer to our own possibilities and worthi-
ness. I am somebody as I become a reflection of the
best of you.

I Just Couldn't

I wanted to tell the whole world
About my love for you
But I just couldn't.
I wanted to dance my love
Sing it or write a poem.
But I just couldn't.

I dreamed a fantastic dream
Of me in your arms
And a long warm kiss.
I wanted the cat to answer me back
When I held her and called your name.
But she just couldn't.

I tried to tell my little sister
About my love for you
So that her big eyes could look at me
The way I want you to.
But she was asleep and so
I just couldn't.

My folks say I'm too young
To be falling in love.

I tried to change my heart
To make my mind stop thinking
About you so much.
But I just couldn't.

I wrote your name on all the pages
of my diary.
I took a letter I wrote you
To the mailbox—
But I just couldn't.

I wanted to shout "Hi Handsome!"
That day after the game
But you were going so fast
And I don't think you saw me.
So I just couldn't.
I couldn't.
I just couldn't.

Evening Lady Lament

Inspired by Dorothy E. King, poet

Look, dear heart,
You are swinging hanging from
Stomping on my
One good nerve here.
How come and
Why is it that when
It's my turn to see you
You got to come high?
Don't talk to me about
Pots and kettles!
All I got is a case of
One glass of wine.
I am together.
Hey no! Don't go!
I'm really glad to see you.
I have waited so long!
Just next time—please, Daddy,
If you got to come high—
Come high on me.

A Real True Love Story

A Duologue

Oh baby, there must be some other way—some
    other man.
Puleeze, Mother dear—
Please don't sound so sad.
I guess if you weren't our only child—
Look! Is it my fault I'm the only child
You and Daddy had?

All our lives we scrimped and planned and worked.
I know how hard you both scrimped and planned and
    worked.
And finally I'm going to marry—
But an ex-con—
Mother! His name is Obadiah!
Obadiah Abdul Brown! Obadiah!
Don't remind me! Sounds like an opportunistic,
    illiterate jerk.
You've got two degrees from the best law school.
Truth, baby, can he read and write?
Of course he can read and write.
He helped me with his defense.

He gave me solid help.
So don't call him names for spite.

I'm trying to just warn you—trying to keep you
    from making—
Mother dear—
Let's put aside all pretense.
Life is just one big chance on a very short ride.
Where is your pride, honey?
It's not my pride that aches.
But why would you want to?
Because I love him, and he loves me!
Love. Love. So?
So I'm going to marry Obadiah.
Love an ex-con, cook, handyman?
Yes! That ex-con, cook, handyman
Is my real true friend besides.
He is a good, good person!

Well, for God's sake is he at least good-looking?
Ugalee, good-looking!
I know he caught my eye.
Mother, he does aawl-l-l the cookin'
And can he bake a pie!
Just what you need, huh, a pie.
Puleeze, Mother dear—
You are grinding on my one good nerve here.

We just want you to marry somebody who—
Do you have to cry?
It's not as if I'm going to die!
Just look at a lotta my friends
Already they got the marital bends,
Clipping coupons, counting pennies,
Concerned about everything from
Eggs to education,
Wondering how they got
In such a stagnant situation,
Doing a lot of wait and wait
Dinner getting stale
Worrying how they rate with some guy
Who's unexpectedly got to work late
Or suddenly gets called to the Bahamas for a business
date,
Smiling through tears
As they tend their little dears.
And if they've got a job too—forget it!
Drop the mop, grab the briefcase
Cook, organize, or try to hire
Bogged down in tasks that never get done.
Comes some special occasion?
Mad scramble from scarecrow attire to business suit.
They got to out-do Houdini to restore some cute.
Hassled on the job, disappointed in bed,
Eyes located all around the head.

Checking things out!
That is not the life for me!
No drowning for me in alcohol, never seeing the girls,
Starving myself, sweating my already tight curls,
Fat farm vacations,
Slit-my-throat temptations.
I'm going to marry a cook, handyman
Who's a real true love by my side.

I think you're overreacting, exaggerating.
Have you checked out his credentials?
Of course I've checked out his credentials!
His potential is—Mother dear, believe me deeply—
In essentials—he's astonishing,
He knows what counts.
He's seen the jive.
I can believe the jive part.
He knows he's lucky to be alive,
Out of jail, finally free.
Don't hold your breath 'til he gets a job!
Well, he's tried for a year to get a realistic nine-to-five,
But I suggested he forget it—that
I could offer him a very good job—Me!
Humph! Without a college education—
No, he's never been to college,
But he's so full of knowledge.
Anyway. Whatever's wrong, I'll help fix.

I've had a few hard licks in my life too, so
We'll just have to help heal, comfort, and strengthen
    each other.
When he gets on his feet—
Stop! Stop it, Mother!
He could leave you so fast.
That's a chance I'll have to take, won't I?
I'll marry him if only for—
For as long as it—
For forever if I can.

But what if he starts to roam?
Think! Maybe he's looking for a home.
Well, Ma, I gotta whole lotta home
Deep inside me
Waiting just for him, and he knows the way.
Now I don't want to wax all lyrical,
But Obadiah is a stone miracle.
The man really knows how to cure whatever ails me.
Ooooh, Muthuh, he just never, never fails me.
Spare me the crude references, please.
Crude? Who? What? Me? Him—crude?
A man who does the laundry, prepares the food.
Promises to help raise the children.
One who adores me with all my dimensions.
I can just let it all hang out without any pretensions.

An understanding, forgiving, one-woman man.
Ooooh, Mother dear, that's why I'm going to marry
       Obadiah
A cook, handyman who is a real true friend by my side.

Some of your friends have traveled abroad.
Made really good matches.
I know that Marie, Angelina, Ruby, Dominique,
       et cetera
Went far away.
Each married a count, a tycoon, an Oba, a sheik,
       et cetera.
You could go to some of those faraway places, too,
       you know.
Oh what the dickens, Muthuh,
I don't want to try the pickings in
Sweden, Germany, Africa, Italy, Greece.
Those places are just too far.
We sisters have to travel to where the brothahs here are.
Where's that—the penitentiary?
What about those very nice singles' weekends in
       the Vineyard?
But those flings for singles, Mother, never made sense!
Whether batting my eyes, flashing my teeth, or
Baring my stark naked intelligence,
There was no stimulating action.

Those folks were in traction.
It all just bored me
And the few precious prize men
Very smoothly ignored me.

I hope you're not just going crazy
over a well-hung pair of pants.
Now that's not fair! I'm not a complete jerk!
There is more to Obadiah than what's in his pants.
Some people who make mistakes, just need another chance.
I've helped to get a lot of people out of the joint.
For years you beat your head against those walls
Why? Why are you doing this—what's the point?
The incarceration system is unfair and needs a lot of
*   work!*
Hey! Some really good and sometimes innocent people get
*   caught in there—*
That's the point.
Mother, Mother—puleeze!
He's going to be the best husband
A busy woman like me could ever have.
Trust me. Obadiah is special.
Too bad he wasn't special enough not to get
    put in there in the first place.
Tell me this, how will he support himself?
What will he use for money?

Mother, as marriages go ours will be nifty.
I'm going to sign a contract with him.
Split my earnings fifty-fifty.
Oh my God!
Mother, Mother,
We'll work things out.
It's not that bad.
I want you to feel good,
Glad for me.
Now when I walk down that aisle
I want you to feel good, to sit up and smile,
To wish me luck,
To say to yourself, to Daddy,
Shout to all our friends,
"Our daughter, her heart and arms and life are full.
Her bed is warm.
She is marrying her love
a cook, handyman
Who is a real true friend by her side."
An ex-con, cook, handyman
Aw come on now, Muthuh!
You will love him.
All I want you to do is say you'll try.
Just say you'll try.
I'll try. I'll try. God knows I'll try.
What's his name?

What are those names?
Mother. Repeat after me. Obadiah.
Obadiah.
Abdul.
Abdul.
Brown.
Brown.
Oh Jesus! Have mercy!

Ode to O.D.

Wait! Ossie wait! After half a century, I have
    something to tell you!
It's been coming together in my head for years.
I've mentioned something of it all before
From time to time in snatches; but I've been
    meaning to make it official.
Write it down.
Give it to you in your hands to hold.
To look at when, from time to time, I seem to lose
    my senses,
To bounce off walls, disorganized,
Distracted, doing ten things at once.
I want you to know
You grab my mind and you steady me,
Help me regain access to myself.

You lift the shades so I can feel the sunshine and
You kiss open my eyes stuck shut
To look at the folly and the contradiction
Between anguishing and prayer.
"You can't insult the power that way.
Once you put out the order,

Plant your plea, you got to water it with some
faith.
Then you got to down it and git from round it,
you say.
"Everything will work out the way it should—
you'll see,"
You say.
And it does.

Wait! I've written it down how over the years.
I've watched your hair, for instance,
Go from black to mint silver;
The way your eyes almost close
From cheeks thrust upward in so much laughing.
The set to those eyes when you're looking and not
listening—
Mind marching in other directions
In rhythms that tell you when to nod or grunt—
Nose that I always want to remind you has places
to get at
Around the nostrils when you wash.
Remember I once showed you and you said
If I wanted to wash your face my way every day
you'd let me?

Sometimes I watch you sleep.
I curl up in your mind and skim titles,

Headlines from the tons of books and papers,
And as you move about and almost smile
I ponder what all else may be in there.
The past or the next chapter of what, of whom?
Mostly you awake so easily and so well
As if Morpheus knows you need to get to
An urgent writing chore at four in the morning.

Your embrace is like warm starless midnights when
Creation cuddles for comfort with familiar forms,
Becomes bulwark against any and all
Demons and destroyers of serenity
Your touch making sure connections
Wired with gentle explosives in series . . .
Broccoli, asparagus, celery, especially breadfruit
Carrots, cucumbers, delicious edible
Realities that hang above or protrude from earth or
Plunge into it, or lay firm along its bosom
Remind me of your magnificent towering
Crowned with tender, exquisite soft sculpture
That maybe the heads of certain mushrooms
Might struggle to imitate.
I love the dark, soft mountains that
Curve to form your shoulders.
Textbook spine.
Hard bulges in buttocks, thighs, calves.
Heels. Marvelous feet.

I imagine myself a lover of horses
Proud of a winning stallion.

Wait! Wait! Ossie, wait.
This day I must gather the scattered notes
Because—
My soul quivers with recognition
Of your grand capacity
To give, to understand, to console, to love—
So much and many people,
But especially me.
So I want to pin a medal, issue a certificate
Notarized, embossed with a stamp,
At a "Let it be known" affair that
I am here in this world with Ossie Davis,
A very good man and a longtime friend,
And I herewith register thanks to
Divine Mother/Father, and Holy Son.

Wait! Wait! Anyhow—here
You'll need your hat against the cold.
And to take off when I am finally down
And all my Ossie documents are finally found.
Hey! Ossie, today is Wednesday!
Trash day!
Don't forget to—to—
Put out the trash.

I Am Somebody

I. I. I say I am. I say I am somebody.
Somebody because—because you—you make me—
    Somebody,
Because—because you are part of
Because you—you share the—the Somebodiness
    of me.

When you laugh, you make my lips a part of
    laughter.
When you cry, tension pulls me from inside.
When you are hungry, my food turns to poison,
    makes me burst
Bony fingers clutch my tongue when I—when I
    know your thirst
Because you are part of—because you—you share the
The Somebodiness of me.

When I see your precious blood out of place, your
    bones exposed in death—
My blood chills and stops as I try to—try to—
    give you breath.
I must keep you from all—all fear and danger—
I must woo your peace of mind—

Help you—help you find joy—
Help you—help you find release
Because you are part of—because you—you share the
    the Somebodiness of me.

I cannot own that which you cannot also possess.
Your crime is mine, and from now on I'll confess
Because you are part of—because you share the
    the Somebodiness of me.

You—you—you are at the other end of the steel
    spring of hate,
So I cannot hate.
When you know my love—my love will warm you—
Cleansing, deep
So, let me—let me take your hand. Let me touch
    your fingers,
Feel your face. Know your heartbeat and all—all
    your doubts erase
Because you are part of—because you—you share the
    the Somebodiness of me.

Falling through
My Arms

❖ ❖ ❖

Some young men—I think of them as my "sons"—
grew up when I wasn't paying attention. I turned
around too late, and they fell through my outstretched arms. Well, not all of them. Some got
caught in other arms or on tree branches. Some are
still falling.

Richard Wesley's play, *The Mighty Gents,* is finely
tuned into these young men's attitudes. When I
saw it I felt a rhythm, a music take over my mind.
I was deeply moved by the beauty and vigor of the
characters, blind though they were to alternatives
and hell-bent for death.

All right. You can't keep people from messing
around with death. "All right. All right," they
seem to be saying. "Why wait for natural conclu-
sions? Let's kill our fool selves today." They act like
a species that won't mind being wiped off the face
of the earth. This attitude expresses itself in other
ways, too.

Early one evening while washing dishes, I heard a
comedian I've since come to respect deliver some
raunchy commentary on television. I mean, it was

low down. Only the rhythm was upbeat. The brother was making a worthy point, but the "how" of it made me drop into a chair. I was shocked. With the television still on, I started making notes that wound up in "Owed to a Funny Man."

Indirectly, I have known some of these restless young men, like Tupac Shakur, the young rap star who was gunned down. His vibes reached me on the ether waves. Ossie and I had met his mother, Afeni Shakur, in the days of the Black Panther Party. She called early one morning. Because Dick Gregory and Ossie chaired the Committee to Defend the Panthers, I assumed she wanted to speak with him.

"Hold on," I said. "I'll get my husband." She replied, "I didn't ask to speak with your husband. I called to speak with you. Can you deal with that?"

I gave the phone to Ossie anyway because I just didn't want to wake up and deal with the struggle at 7:30 a.m. But the memory sticks in my mind. Now I tell myself, "Tornadoes, fires, and revolutions won't wait 'til you put on your makeup and have your morning coffee, Ruby."

The Mighty Gents

Street dreamers, the Mighty Gents
Used-to-be adolescents
Huddle together in final
Old gang warmths where
False dream clouds solidify into
Psychedelic hatchet sharpness
To a boomerang beat.
Noses and arms and fingers still
Thrust through solid city air and
Grope for brass rings.

Fulfillment dreams—
Spawned by unintelligible economies
By the gangster class
By religious hems and haws
By the respectable corrupt
By ineffectual classroom rituals
By sick and tired middle class
By daddies who didn't know and
By mamas who couldn't stop them
Dreams that guarantee only early
Rigor mortis—
Clang spastically in heads

Messed up, too, by ladyfingers
Cowboy flicks with gunslingers
Taming frontiers, slaves, Indians,
God, anything.

Street dreaming Mighty Gents
Mark time with jingles
Wine bottles and rusty needles.
Nervous eyes grab at the
Golden garbage of wealth
Triumph in falling down drunk
With no bones broke and in
Struggling up for one more step
One more snort, or for
Diamond cuff links so "I can
Be forever."

Gimme five 'cause tha's the way it
Bees and
Look out for number one and
If I don't, who else is gonna, and
Ain't that what freedom is all about?
Not to be tied down no how
Bound nowhere to nobody and nothing.
Except—hey yeah—remember
The Mighty Gents! "Street Dreamers!"

Then comes cool greed with
Bullet eyes to collect, to
Dislodge flesh, shatter bones, and
What remains of dwarfed-in-the-first-place
Solid friendships and deep dreams.

The Mighty Gents now sport stillness.
Fat rats immune to death
Descend quicksand steps to gnaw on cold flesh
Propped up ramrod straight
In final indignity.
No babies come here so
Hope renewed doesn't stand a chance.
But one of their women
Cries.

Go On

Go on. Go on. Go on. Go on.
Pop plunge pluck pull pitch
Pop plunge pluck pull pitch
Pop plunge pluck pull pitch
Go on
Pop dat pill
Plunge dat needle
Pluck dat baby
Pitch dat bomb
Peep it, pal
Peoples isn't necessary nohow.

Owed to a Funny Man

A Duet—With thanks to James Weldon Johnson

"Lift every voice and sing
'Til earth and heaven ring—"

Born of the dead where
The beat was in but
The vital substance had fled
Had run screaming through
The centuries, the decades, the years
Beaten, chased, squeezed
Castrated, teased
Raped, robbed, ridiculed
Pistol on the brain exploding,
"Gotcha, nigger. Gotcha. Die. Die. Die."

Bright, bright, bright boy
Knew the beat alright but
Never heard the song.

Disconnected since the womb days
Mama on maintenance arrangements
No time, no space, no equipment for

The kindergarten of who, what
When, where, why, how of I/us
You/them/me my country 'tis of thee
Let alone the lessons
Of the history lessons.

The beat had got boxed in
Trapped in too many
Editorials, cartoons
Movies, plays, downright lies
Amos 'n' Andy, crow, coon.
Ugly faces barred behind too many injustices
Too many criminals in high places
Couldn't even hear the song.

"We have come over a way that with tears has been
        watered,
Treading a path through the blood of the
        slaughtered."

Bright, bright, bright boy
Couldn't even hear the song.

Becomes minstrel in paint, minus pain
Demon in chocolate with flashing teeth
Self-winding computer toy
Heart, soul, hanging by a thread

Almost-zombie boy with
Jack o'lantern funny flicker
Bloodless, Hallowe'en inside
Cool essence of self-negation
Brutalization, indifference
Contempt streamlined.
Stereotype personified.
Expert in black on black cancellation
Tangled in the sleek new slave chains
That clang with every step, "Kill yourself, nigger.
Tired of killing you.
And while the job is getting done, here is
All the gold you can pocket,
All the rides, genu-wine leather
To plaster on your bulging thighs."
Yeah! Cheers to the foul-mouthed champs
Dealing in crotch with diamonded hands as
Eyes, cheap beads, glisten from empty sockets—
And mouth minus lips curls around
Idiot four letter screams and
Messed up mind
Thinks it thinks:
"Simple-minded shit heads
I will kill myself m—f—s!
On stage!
Then I will kill you!
Make you drink my sewered blood and die!"

One night I dreamed I was his mother:
"Get down from there and
Don't make me
Have to come get you."
Took charge of that stage
Scraped off jeweled pants
Before mindless/bloodless fans
Cheering on the deaths—his and theirs—and
Switched him with a triple-thick hickory all over.
Snatched him off the poisoned pedestal.
Flung him into the arms of the decontamination
      delegation—
All the weeping mamas, teachers, daddies,
      divinities
All the crucified Jesuses—
"Come here to us, boy.
You are sick. Far from funny.
We will wash your mouth out.
We will take you searching for
Your stolen and misplaced parts.
We mean to unscramble you but good."

*"Lest our feet stray from the places, our God, where we
      met Thee."*

What you mean, zombie son?

*"Lest our hearts drunk with the wine of the world,
    we forget Thee."*

Skipping all the black songs that go with the
    black beats
All the black people who died, who died—
People who died—
So you could—go to school
People who died—
So you could—hold your head up again
Who died—
So you could—get a good job
Who died—
So you could—be able to vote
Who died—
So you could—not get wasted on a whim.

Who are your folks? Don't you *love* nobody?
Letting yourself become rat-impaled on the nail of
    racism
Begging to justify extermination
How dare you mess with your people's expectations
People who died—
So you could—explore heights
Who died—
So you could—be your best self, show your good
    stuff

Who died—
So you could—live in peace in this land
People who died who died who died
So you could so you could so you could
People who died so you could
People who died so you could
Be a credit to your race
People who died so you could
People who died so you could
Be a credit to the human race.

You got people who love you.
People who got to love you
Got to love you
Got to love you
Got to love yourself
Love ourselves
Love yourself.

Move. Move over. Move out.
While we tear down this stage
We got to build a new place
"God of our weary years—"
Where you can—
Hear the old songs then
Write some new songs
"God of our silent tears—"

Where you can—feel the old beats then
Teach some new beats
"Thou who has brought us thus far on the way"
Where you can begin to be about—
Caring about people who look up to you
"May we forever stand. True to our God."
Begin to be about
Our purpose on this earth
Begin to be about
Our dimensions so long hidden
Too long overlooked and trampled on
"True to our God"
Begin to be about
Our exalted dimensions to come.
"We have come over a way that with tears has been
    watered—"
People who died so you could people who died
    so you
Could people who died so you could . . .

Tupac

Tupac. Womb walked with
The warriors. The nation
Builders who believed
They could make a difference who
Made special rules who
Wore special hats who
Took special names who
Set up special schools who
Tried to feed some of the hungry
Take responsibility
Take charge of their lives
Their communities.

Tupac. Came after
In aftermath
Tupac. Child of the self-made
Cut down warriors
Trails memories and sounds of
Death lessons tattooed in the
Buildings and in the foreheads of his
Mamas and daddies and
Big eyes swallowed some deep truths
Before brains got time to get in gear.

Grows up out loud
Sometimes wrong but searching.

Not knowing that the word's been out for years:
Okay. Grow up but quiet. Sing. Dance.
Do your weed.
C.E.O. it, even. Play ball.
But that revolution thing. We don't
Do that—no mo'.
Any number of ways to—like—
Get with it. Get over. Get down.
F—— revolution. F—— thinking.
Get yourself some money.
Get with a gang.
Be a star. Actor, rapper, athlete,
Or the new town clown.
Revolutionaries don't get job security.
They compete with rats for cheese and
With strays for shelter after the
Big bullets make feet out of their knees.

Tupac.
Spelled backwards—
Caput. Meaning
Finished. Over. Ended. Done.
Twenty-six was it?
Oh my God. So young
Mouths drop. Stop in
Unbelieving anguish and surprise
And from dry eyes
Tears cascade inside.

Mostly Laughing

❖ ❖ ❖

In one form or another, humor has always been a
part of the human struggle. It's the great equalizer,
the grease in the wheel. There is danger in humor,
too, when it discounts aspirations, struggle, or history. It used to be easier to tell when something
was funny. I would laugh. But some of the so-
called funny stuff I hear today makes me want to
cry—or makes me mad as hell.

Finding good humorous or satirical material to
perform is tough, particularly if I want it to be
about black people. There are so many more serious pieces. Yet all audiences appreciate a good
laugh. And black people need one more than most.
So whenever the spirit moves me, I write something humorous myself. I'm grateful for the example of Mother Goose, Langston Hughes, Zora Neale
Hurston, Mark Twain, Yip Harburg, Ossie, and
humorists like Dick Gregory and performers like
Moms Mabley. Among such illustrious madness,
I find a nest for my own fledgling brand of humor.

Take Langston Hughes. He dropped by my brain
one day in the form of one of his favorite characters, Jesse B. Simple. Jesse jumped up off the pages

of the book and asked me if I needed another brother. I said yes. I fell in love with him. After Langston died and left all of us for good, Simple wanted to keep on expressing himself. "Hughes can't walk out on me like this after all our years together. I wasn't finished talking yet!" That's how I came to write the Simple stories. I hope Langston approves.

Humpty Dumpty

Humpty Dumpty, huh?

Humpty Dumpty sat on a wall
Humpty Dumpty had a great fall
They say he fell
But you know and I know and history
Will prove—
That Humpty was pushed.
And all the king's horses and some of
Humpty's kin
Lynched him and shot him
And killed him again.

Compare

The pocketbook
And body snatchers
Masked
Desperate
Terrible creatures
Sneaking through the night
Are as babies

Compared to
The correctly suited
Easy smiling
Thieves
And killers of our world
Dealing through the day.

Some People!

Some people! Oh Gawd!
They got no sense and
They don't know shame.
What to do?
Who is to blame?
They get out of bed
Put on a few clothes
Then come shine or come rain
Talking all up in somebody's nose
Flaunting they smooth and naked brain.

Shoe Lady #1

There izzan old lady who lives in a shoe
Doesn't have any children
Cause she knew what to do
Swallowed birth control pills her young life
    through
Scraped out and aborted quite another few.
In corporate glory she reached for the ring
Rode high on the hog and did her own thing
'T'was on account of cut-blacks her misfortunes
    grew
Today she is crying—boo-hoo, boo-hoo
'Cause
She's all by herself in that lonely ol' shoe.

Shoe Lady #2

There wuzzan old lady who lived in a shoe.
Had so many children (thirteen, to be exact)
And she did all she knew to do.
She and her husband scrimped and scraped
Cleaned them and fed them and sent them to
    school.
           But
Four got killed in an undeclared war,
Two got shot in a scrape with the law,
She lost some more to the needle trade,
One disappeared while in the first grade,
One worked in politics, got to be mayor
(See how the Lord does answer prayer!)
The family no longer sings the blues
Because—
The mayor condemned rentals of sneakers and
    shoes.

Now the rest of the children, mother and spouse
All live together in a pretty nice house.

Shoe Lady #3

Wuzza third ol' lady who lived in a shoe
Had so many children—
And it was a very crowded situation!
Her husband died from asbestosis
And with the insurance money
She moved out and got a lovely apartment.
Then came the de-controls and
Her building turned into luxury condos.
She couldn't afford $1500. A month plus!
So,
With all those children she had to *bus* back to that
    shoe
Which was, by then, subdivided into rooms.
So now
This ol' lady lives in the *toe* of a shoe
Children packed in like sardines, trying not to
    breathe
Whispering:
    "Mama, this is ridiculous.
    Isn't there someplace else we can go?
    Do you want people to say,
    'There was an old lady who lived in a *toe*?'"

Jack and Jill

Jack and Jill
Moved up on a hill
To get away from the slaughter
And things were going real swell until
A minority married their daughter.

To Pig or Not to Pig

"I am in the doghouse now," said Simple. "Let me take that back. The truth of the matter is that I am under the doghouse, if I am not the mangy dog."

"Why's that?" asked the bartender.

"Well, the other day I brought home some pork chops and Joyce started in on me. Made me so mad yak yakking about this and that, and that if I don't lay off my pork chops, I'm gonna get a case of cholesterol, turn to worms, and die with a heart attack."

"Lots of people are giving up the hog and trying to eat less meat altogether. Raw food seems to be the big thing now," ventured the bartender.

"Now you bad as Joyce," said Simple. "What I look like walking up to a raw cow and taking a bite."

"You know I don't mean raw cow. Although some people do eat raw cow. Of course, it's all ground up with onions and spices. It's called steak tartare. However, I was referring mostly to raw vegetables."

"Refer on," said Simple. "Like I told Joyce, I do not like and will not eat raw vegetables or any other kind of rabbit food. I know I'll die from something, so it may as well be from something I love like pork chops—fried, then smothered in onions with gravy or baked in a roast with tomatoes and little potatoes swimming on the side. It is better to die with your stomach happy than to be hit by a truck or to poison myself just breathing. And then she hit on my ignorance. I say it's my ignorance so just leave it alone."

"Stubbornness or ignorance is a bad thing," said Joyce, "so you just take your chops back to the store or else cook them yourself."

"Now, I am not too good in the kitchen," Simple continued, "but a wise man does not let a woman think he can't do for himself if he has to. I just told her to move on out the way. I'd cook my own damn chops. Then she come pushing me out the kitchen, saying I can't cook no pig parts in her pots because she would have to decontaminate everything. Then I did it again. I asked her, 'You got anything to decontaminate your ugly, mean self? Look in the mirror and you'll see that you and my pork chops have a lot in common. You both come from pig.'"

"That was an unforgiveable thing to say. How can you possibly call her ugly?" asked the bartender. "Joyce is a fine-looking woman."

"I know it," said Simple. "She is *my* woman. True, she is not ugly, but Gawd a'mighty she *can* be mean at times. Let me teach you something, my man. When you don't have all night and you need to win an argument real fast, just call *any* woman ugly and you got it made."

"It's a wonder she didn't hand you your head."

"No, she just sat down, swelled up, and started crying. I told her I was sorry and to please forgive me, but she wouldn't say nothing. Just steady crying. I felt bad. I said, 'Okay, Joyce, I don't have to have those chops. Come on, Baby, let me take you out to eat.'

"She said, 'But I already fixed our dinner. It's in the icebox. Then she whipped into action. Set the table and brought out this big bowl of cold raw vegetables arranged like some kind of flower. First we had some soup with little scraps of chicken in it, and then we ate gobs and gobs of that vegetation. Oh, she liked that. She even apologized for screaming at me about my ignorance. Said she did it because she loves me and hates to think of my veins getting clogged up with cold fat, because she wants me to live and be with her always. Said if I just had to have some pig, maybe she'd cook me some pig liver New Year's Eve.' "

"Sounds like you made a good compromise," said the bartender. "For your own good, I might add."

"Wait, now, let me tell you the rest," said Simple. "You see, late that night, when I thought Joyce was asleep, I got hungry, got up, got my chops ready and put them in the pan to cook. I guess I must have dozed off, because the next thing I knew, look like the stove had caught fire and Joyce was hollering, 'Get the baking soda. Open the windows.' Oh the smoke was everywhere, and Joyce burnt her hand getting rid of my burnt chops, and then the phone started ringing and people come banging on the front door. What got me, though, was when I heard the fire truck. If the house was on fire—"

"It's comforting to know that the fire department responded so quickly—especially in Harlem," interrupted the bartender.

"Now I don't know what to do. Since that little grease fire, Joyce stopped speaking to me. Hasn't said a word to me in two days."

"I can see you are in trouble. Would you consider telling her that you'll ease into eating raw vegetables, if she'll cook you some chops, say, maybe, once a month? It's cold in the doghouse, I imagine," suggested the bartender.

"Eating like that is asking an awful lot from love," said Simple. "I started writing her a song, though, and soon's I finish it, I'm gon' sing it to her. It's called 'Don't Let Pig Part True Love.'"

"That might make matters worse," said the bartender.

"Oh, no," said Simple, "Joyce likes it when I hold her and sing softly in her ear."

Honkies Is a Blip!

"Honkies is a blip!" said Simple.

"I haven't heard that word in a long time," said the bartender as he put a brew down for his sometime favorite customer.

"Which word?" asked Simple. "You are at least as old as I am, and I am somewhere up there with Methuselah. Why you want to pretend you do not remember the word blip?"

"Hold it," said the bartender, "I was referring to your use of the word *honky*."

"Well how am I supposed to use it?"

"I mean if you are referring to white people as *honkies*—that word is almost as passé as *blip*."

"Well past A or past B, I'm gon' use them. I'll bring 'em back. Start a old trend or something."

"Do you like it when white folks refer to us as niggers?"

"What I don't like is when they lump all people of color under that name when being a nigger has nothing to do with color!"

"Hold it. Back up. There you go again," said the bartender. *"They. They.* What *they*? What about when we call each other niggers?"

"Don't try to change the subject," said Simple. "I am talking about *honkies*. The honkies are turning all kinds of people—white people especially—into hat-ducking, slavery-time niggers."

"You are talking about powerlessness. I think you are using the word *nigger* to describe those who are made to feel inferior, who have lost confidence in their ability to change the conditions of their lives—to make them more meaningful."

"Yeah, that's it," said Simple. "You feel like nobody loves you, useless and helpless, especially when you get laid off and you have to wait a lot in some kind of long line."

"From your definition, all *honkies* are not white either," said the bartender.

"I buy that. One of the biggest honkies I know is my landlady," laughed Simple. "And believe me, wherever you find honkies, you will find niggers and vice versa. They go together."

"I'm listening," said the bartender.

"You see," explained Simple, "a honkie just cares about himself. He thinks he is superior. But he is mostly a habitual thief—stealing something all the time—somebody else's country, for instance, and trying to keep the take hid in a big Swiss bank. Then, some of them say, 'Y'all keep order there while us honkies do the important, big-man work of making progress all over the place.' The trouble is, they keep on progressing and messing up everything everywhere they go. Anything to turn a dollar. Just look at upstate New York, where the honkies sold those houses built on top of that poisoned garbage. I bet those niggers don't know the half of what is going on. I do not want to worry about anyone using my life to shoot craps for 'progress'—like those niggers scrambling around shaking and worrying over that nuclear life-improvement scheme in Pennsylvania," impassioned Simple.

"All life involves risk," countered the bartender. "For example, almost every phase of development—say in science or technology—has what is called 'an acceptable kill ratio.'"

"Acceptable to who? See, when honkies don't have to get your permission to put your ass on the line, you are a stone *nigger*. But the biggest thing honkies do is keep the niggers divided. White niggers, black niggers, brown yellow red niggers—you get a lot of people hating each other, beating, shooting, cutting, killing, and scraping on each other, fighting over bones and paying more and more for everything without even chunking a brick or

87

something—like it's God Himself who keeps on raising prices. Sometimes niggers all over the world forget why they fighting each other. They just keep on fighting, crying, and dying. Fighting, crying, and dying. I think it must be getting good to 'em! They be praying to God to help 'em. If I was God, I'd tell 'em, say, don't put my name in that! Get together! That will consist of your salvation. And don't think I'm gon' let you off by just destroying the whole shebang. That would be too easy! Or for the stupidity of not getting together, I will consign you to hell—the hell of keeping on going the way you are!"

"See honkies," continued Simple, "know that their smart-alecky ignorance has come full circle and doubled back some; but the bluff is in, so they keep niggers the world over crawling and scrambling all over each other trying to figure what their next smart move is gon' be about."

Simple didn't say anything for a while as he finished his brew. The bartender brought him another.

"That it? You sure you've said all you had to say on the subject? That's your definition of the word *honky?*"

"Yeah," said Simple. "Don't you agree with me? Come on. Let's say it together. Honkies is a blip."

"That word *blip*—you got me there. If I knew what it meant, I've forgotten," said the bartender.

"Blip," said Simple, "is what you say because the word that honkies really is is so terrible the devil himself is 'shamed to say it."

Tributes

❖ ❖ ❖

The world has improved mostly because unorthodox people did unorthodox things. Not surpris-
ingly, they had the courage and daring to think
they could make a difference. They weren't prone
to measure their energies. They weren't likely to
live by equations.

To the risk takers, the wise ones, I say, "We
embrace you; we need you. If you were to die,
we would not be ready. We would cry as if you
were blood relatives." Malcolm X, for example,
told us over and over that certain forces were
about to claim his life. Is there nothing we could
have done to protect him? Couldn't we have spir-
ited him away? Shielded him with our many bodies? Deflected the bullets? Howled to heaven for
his life?

And I remember Diana Sands. When Lloyd
Richards, the director, first asked me to read the
play, *A Raisin in the Sun,* I was sure the part he had
in mind for me was the rebel, Beneatha. To my
deep disappointment, he wanted me to play her
sister-in-law, Ruth, a much less dynamic character.
"The role of Ruth has its rewards, and it is difficult," Lloyd assured me. "I absolutely need you to

play it." I had no thought of turning it down, but when I met Diana, I felt her electricity and knew immediately why Lloyd had cast her as Beneatha. She became like another baby sister. Then, suddenly, she, too, was gone forever.

I frequently write tributes to people I admire or cannot stop thinking about. Roger Furman and James Van Der Zee chronicled Harlem's rhythms and passions in never-to-be-captured-again times. Lionel Hampton, also Harlem-based, left his mark not only with his music, but in the impressive, affordable Gladys Hampton Houses on Eighth Avenue. Clara Hale, like Mamie Phipps Clark, was head and heart deep in children. Carolyn M. Rodgers and Toni Cade Bambara gave us deeply satisfying literature to read aloud and share. I still haven't written all the word-portraits of those who have inspired me.

Sometimes people drift through my life, and I put them on hold with the mental note, "Get to Know Better By and By." Some tributes take more thinking about than others. Some almost write themselves.

For James Baldwin

Drums, tom-toms from ancient times filled the
    cathedral
We took off our clothes and the benches marched
    themselves to walls
And we danced in circles to the rhythm of the
    drums
Around the body of James Baldwin and
In the forest his words broke through the drums.
We looked up as we danced, waving feathers
Shaking bells, and cowry shells, pounding sticks
While we beat the earth with our feet.
Mother in wheelchair and smooth-faced children
All danced around the bier.

Amiri and Toni and Maya and Paule and Odetta
    sang "Kum Ba Yah"
Then we danced all night in the forest of
    somebody's apartment.
And sung the slave songs and wept and shouted
    and laughed and
Drank scotch on the rocks and smoked cigarettes
And we put on our Jimmy masks with pop eyes
    and spacey teeth and

The laugh—and filled up from deep inside with
    his greatness.
At dawn we saw him take a last drag on his smoke,
Strike that pose and then turn and leave
And the tom-toms slowed.

Essayist, playwright, novelist, friend, and brother
A Baldwin spirit shaped like Jimmy became part
    of the ether
As we watched out the windows as far as our eyes
    could follow.
Then when we reached back for our clothes
We found them wet with the tears of the people
    who stood behind us
Still singing of the life that is a song of us
Of all of us in pain, in praise, in love
And in challenge.

He had spelled out some of the complexities
Had put the struggle in perspective.
Yeah! He wedded us to some clarities too!
Finally we closed rank around our memories and
We gathered up the strewn feathers
Lion's teeth and pieces of elephant heart
And went slowly on back home.

Elders and Partisans

Thank God for the passionate partisans
Those fiercely on our side
They snatch us to attention, focus and define
    the nature of the tide.
We're thankful too for the court jesters
    (outrageous clowns)
Skilled in announcing to the emperor
That his pants is hanging down.
We even need those in ugly opposition—
    (just a few)
Above all we need those with a sense of history
Armed with that long and steady view
To join the struggle, help map the righteous fight
    and win
Without the brave committed always getting
    treacherously done in.

For Roger Furman

Founder of the New Heritage Theatre in Harlem

It is not always easy to define the extraordinary
To describe essences exactly—
It is like measuring devotion or
Like clocking the rhythm of a community—
A community like Harlem.

When Harlem touches a life
Sometimes that life opens up
Enfolds the place
And locks it within forever.

Through the years, artists—
Painters/poets/musicians/dancers/actors/writers—
Tell us something about
The Harlem embrace and about belonging.
Roger Furman—
An eternally new-to-the-world kind of person—
Was one of those who
Understood some of the whats and hows of that
     belonging—
Why so many thrilled and enthralled to the special
     embrace

From which great vantage point
It could become clear how things ought to be
Or ought to be changed
In the rest of the world.

And Harlem gave way to the Roger configurations
Was comfortable being worn by him
Like a living overcoat
Trusted him in the opening up of its nooks and
     crannies and secret spaces
Respected his observations and his interpretations
On stage, in movies, in a classroom
Anywhere.

Roger Furman—
Jaunty spring-stride in headgear
That seemed to grow from his head
Was a faithful and passionate love
Of Harlem. Of the people there.
He recognized its intangible glories
Penetrated the particular atmosphere
Deftly selecting spices for his New Heritage
     Theatre
Or for his life or for
The lives of those needing Harlem's special
     nurture.
He could direct us to Harlem's nectars of joy

He knew the pulses of pain there and
Told us about coming from way down deep
Under the scheme of tough times
To move on through to the "up" side
And keep on trucking.

Distance fogs reasons for devotions.
What made/makes Harlem defy the definitions
Why did/do we call it great?
Furman. That's some of the answer.
The splendor and elegance of spirit
Of people like Roger Furman.

The Photographer

James Van Der Zee.
Man with box on wooden legs
Praise the Lord
He lived to
Chronicle our lives
In photographs capturing
Black grace, Black pride, Black struggle
Strut, ceremony, and aspiration.

Taking pictures through box on legs
To chronicle a time,
Streets and houses and people—
Children, brides and grooms, and
Politicians, educators, poets, preachers
Dancers. Housewives in kitchens.
In photographs.

He makes us see some of
Who we were
Who we are
How we change
How we stay the same

Through a box on wooden legs with
Black drape cloth
No need to trade it for the
Ever newer models.
Van Der Zee—careful. Slowly
Needed to come through the box
And fuse his understanding and his love with
The points of focus.

Needed a very special look
Certain kind of light
On the stories he had to tell
So that they would be distinctive.
Remembered. Aglow with the
Innerness of our waiting-to-be
Heralded glory.
James. James Van Der Zee.

Artist. Photographer with box on legs.
Praise the Lord!
He lived.

George Houston Bass

He was like a son to Langston Hughes
Guardian of his legacy as
Offspring of High John de Conqueror
Whose historical reality
Zora Neale Hurston mapped and set down.

Ancestor who walked on water
Became water by the dipperful too
To ease parched tongues and
To bless the babies.

Ancestor with wings
Moving among the tribes to comfort
To summon to convention for
Strategy planning for the journey's
Next lap through the white madnesses.

Ancestor with throat wide for
The laughter and the song that
Prevented pain from completely taking over—
Boot sock and soul.

Ancestor with a warm and sure embrace
For the peacekeeping, lovemaking,
Forgiving chores.

Ancestor, building and mending bridges
Making narrower ugly gaps too wide
To jump in consciousness and understanding.

Zora told us George was coming
Descended from High John who lives forever
And he came—
Offspring of "a bottom fish"
And like Zora
"He was deep."

Lionel Notes

Among whom the gods bless
High high on the list
Are the music people—
Tuned in to celestial vibrations
To give mortals a taste
Of immortal sensations.

The Universe pulses
The music soul carves out
Picks up translates brings down
The beat.

With drums strings
Pipes and Lionel Hampton's
Little hammers on the vibes
To complete circles
Ease squares
Draw good angles.

. . . Hamp bees sharp
Beams thanks
Knows paradise is to be

Ultimate instrument
Eraser of fears
Gateway for divine fulfillments
Heavy intents
To be
Love connection for hungry ears.

So he serves
Climbs political boulders for
Better housing to transform
Rundown streets
Finger popping laughing little angels
. . . From his head down to his feets.

Brings into present tense sessions
With the boys
In nightclubs, concert halls—wherever
Glories of remembered trips
On earth
In heaven
With Gladys
And then
Flying home
Leaves us all
Soaring too
Laughing out loud
In the shimmering silences.

Mamie Phipps Clark

"We can't do that to the children," she said.
Gentle, elegant, determined lady
Part of beauty, beauty part of her
We saw that she came from refinement
Advantages.
Loved music and poetry
Loved children.
She especially loved the children
From the streets and from
Broken homes and from
Lives broken in ways that
Cities and calloused circumstances
Can break bodies and minds.
She lent her throat to form the screams
"We can't do that to the children," she said.

Even her dreams embraced their hurts
And put on flesh.
Feet followed the North Star and
Founded the Northside Community Center
Founded a model of service
And welcome for the damaged children
For the damaged parents

For the damaged potential
"We can help undo this damage!" she said.

Gentle, delicate lady with daring flexibilities
Fine-tuned in on right and wrong
Straddled the chasms between the haves and have-nots
Built bridges for the necessary transfers
Guided the lovers and givers through
Mazes of doubts and technicalities
Broke barriers between uptown and downtown.
Inserted new backbone in the bent over children and
Hacked to pieces the "Nothin's gonna happen"
    syndrome
Of the smirkers and the self-doubters.
"We can't do that to the children!" she said.

And the Northside Center for Child Development
    rose,
Grew strong, confident
Prospered from slum surrounding to modern elegance.
In Mamie Phipps Clark
Active serenity mapped plans and programs
Drawn with the efficiency of an expert and
The tender care of the beginner
Plans and programs
For child development, for enriching the children

For promoting the promise, for protecting the
    family
For weeding out "no" to life
Teaching the difference between pretense and
    productivity
Glitter and gold
Talk and commitment
Teaching the High Court the
High crime against the heart and the mind
Inherent in disguises and doctrine of "Separate but
    Equal."
"You can't do that to the children," she said.

Mamie Phipps Clark
A melody among us
Presence beyond intellect among us
Wife entwined with living man among us
Mother, sister, friend among us
Volumes on love among us
Was with us. Is with us still.
Like a prompter in the wings
Urging us to reach out with love to
The children. The children.
The children who
Hold in their hearts and hands
Our measure, our future
Ourselves.

All That Love

Somebody must have truly adored Clara Jane
From a teeny tot an awful lot
Growing up her folks must have really
Piled on pride, then made her
    Tough, able to keep in balance
    On a high held head
    All that love.
And it multiplied.

One day a daughter of all that love
Brought home an addicted mother and her
    newborn child
(Spaced-out baby that
The Right to Life folks
Maybe haven't heard about or
They would do much more about
What kind of life the unborn have
The right to anyway.)
Said, "Mama there's a whole lotta
Ladies with babies need a love fix."
So, Clara Jane and husband and the
Children became conductors on the
Street-ground railroad for trembling

Tots born of trembling mamas.
All that love got a real workout
Finding the money for food and
Clothes and things.
All that love had to talk fast and smile much
For just a little more space.

Clara Jane got to be Mother Hale
    to the sidewalk people
Got over the bureaucrats who said
She couldn't do what she was doing
Not legal—all those babies and
In one small apartment without a permit.
No, Clara Jane said, "I'm not a professional, but
    I believe
I qualify. You see, when they first come to me,
I rub their limbs and rock them and we
Walk and I talk to them, day and night
'Til they stop crying and calm down some.
I tell them they have to get well,
Everybody's waiting for them to grow up
To be about whatever business the Lord
Wanted them born for in the first place."

And the crying, twitching, aching babies
Began coming from all over recommended by
Her own children and neighbors and

Hospitals and government agencies who said
"We're not prepared to handle this sort of thing—
Our facilities can't accommodate one more—
Call that woman—What's her name?—Mother
    Hale?
You know, the woman with all that love who says—"
"We make sure they know we need them.
We make sure they look at themselves in all these
    mirrors
So they can see that what we tell them is true
That they are beautiful.
By and by, they come to know, you see, that
We truly love them."

And Clara Jane McBride Hale
Mother Hale, the woman with
All that love
Puts a bottle in another new mouth and smiles.

Toni Cade Bambara

Toni Cade Bambara
Bamba, Bamba, Bambara
Toni Cade Bambara
Even her name a heartbeat
Ancient woman
Voodoo priestess with pen
Magna cum laude in
The politics of essential
Considerations.
Woman-to-woman
Sistuh-to-sistuh to
Child to husband to lover to
Family to government systems
To world to universe discovered
And undiscovered.

Technical,
Mind going every whichaway
In scary, funny, foot-patting
Order.

Coming at deep from way
Down under deep

No stone unturned where
Love might be or where
Snakes hide.

Bamba, Bamba, Bambara
Toni Cade Bambara
Even her name a harmony
Soul dancer
Gold medal acrobat on
World brain bars.
Black goddess of connections
Riding hard and fast
On a miracle mule to
The far corners and to
All the spaces in between
Shaping ether.
Touching everything everywhere
Matching moments for all
Sorts of history to establish
New rhythms
Sanctify some old ones and
To throw wide open the doors
On the supply places
Housing the stuff to live by.
Making "Uh-Humm" the heaviest
Word in the dictionary.
Doing the world's necessary

"Spade" work to a pick-ax beat
A "Lady Day" blues
And a laugh that rescues beauty and
Truth from the tight spaces
The nasties have crammed it into.

Bamba, Bamba, Bambara
Toni Cade Bambara
Nurturer.
Life epitomized.
Handle on hope.
Black woman.

Thinking about
Carolyn M. Rodgers

With wide smile in Giacometti skull face
Or with fat hot tears flaming
Down hollow cheeks
And with fingers (little bones) pushing heavy
    pencils
Or blurring on salvaged junkheap typewriter
This exclamation point poet
Using self for sword
Goes screaming with glee—
Arms scare-crowed out
Flapping for embrace
Rustling minds
Scatting death from necrotic souls
Dueling with madness
To win some order for all our sakes.

Thinking about Diana Sands

Diana, Diana, Diana
Dear, dear Diana, Diana
    Thanks for giving us this little time
    To contemplate the essences.
    To spike the search
    To say "easy now" to fears.

Dear, dear Diana, Diana
    You skipped the rest of the questions.
    I see you now kick off your shoes
    And wink at the unfathomable
    Because now you know for sure
    Forever all the answers.

Oh Diana, dear, dear Diana
    I know you know the right turns now.
    Certain now you have the antidote
    To frustration
    To the spastic pursuit.

I want to know the secret
   I long to hear your *now* advice.
   Is there fulfillment in the "keep
       on keepin' on?"
   How today can art redeem—
   Clarify the horizon line.

Diana, Diana, Diana, dear Diana
   Whisper to me, sister.
   I've seen you rage and tremble
   Torn with anxiety as you try, cry, try
   On stage, on camera, on life
   And when I listen for you
   I hear deep soul laugh
   And watch your full mouth
   Form a smile.
   Why?
   Whisper to me, sister.

For My Brother-in-Law, Bill Morgan

In all the years—
I could count on ten fingers perhaps
The times we've sat and talked a while.
At those few times, though, I glimpsed through you
A kind of Black Man that I've known forever.

Mostly they wait in dim-lit places,
Their presence intensifying shadows
Backgrounding hurts and screams
Becoming bounce-back off walls
Of cave after cave after cave.

Deep creased, chisled faces—
Bony men with large hands
To extend across chasms
Big feet moccasined for silently tracking the
    troubled
Tough hard shoulders and long-muscled
Strong arms angled to comfort and to embrace
Quiet, slow, soft speech—just enough
Quickened sometimes with a glass of wine

Laughter sometimes—low and almost apologetic
Deep gleam from steady eyes
Reflecting the tears of centuries
Crystallized to determinations:
>   Not to feel the current lashes
>   To act as shield
>   To undergird bottoms
>   To become open pit for pain and
>   Springboard to the feeling-better times.

Yes, dear brother-in-law, you suggest some
>   Black Men I've known
From schoolrooms, or prisons, or pulpits
From families or histories—
Who seem to ease out of the shadows of the ages
To come and live among us gently for a while.

Sarah and John—
We Think of Them Together

As it was in the past, so be it now,
Sarah and John together.
Struggle in human form, the living, beating heart,
The conscience of the cause
Two sheltering rocks against the wind forever
To whom the least could always turn, and turn
    again.
Two lights in a large and single welcome window,
Good coffee, good laughing, and crying, too.
A buck to fit your pocket if you needed— —
A hand for helping out
Advice. Comfort. Strength to fight
And fall, rise to fight again, against
Race hate and anti-Semitism and McCarthyism,
And lynchings, and children hurt, and not enough
    bread on some
Working body's table, and people with no names
    and no jobs.

Sarah and Sarah's John, we see them together.

We stumble now because our loss is heavy, but love,
and struggle,
And Sarah herself has taught us something:
Stumble yes, but the march itself continues,
Don't break rank, join hands, and keep the line
moving,
Pick up the banner, pass the torch forward,
Take up the sword that fell, fill the space she left
With working men and women, but always
Join hands, and keep the line moving.
In her name, and in her spirit, in every language
conceivable to the human heart,
Say what Sarah's dauntless, fighting heart always said:
No pasaran . . .
Say what Langston Hughes always said:
We have tomorrow bright before us like a flame.
Yesterday, a night-gone-thing, a sun-down name.
And dawn today broad arch above the road we came.
We march!

Sarah, and Sarah's John, we think of them together—
We always will—so
Don't break rank, join hands, and keep the line
moving.

For Marvin Gaye

I never saw you face to face
Or attended too much to the
Kinds of songs you sang
But I shuddered through the grapevine
When I heard you died
And reached to touch the empty *space*.

I miss you
From out the corner of my eye.

Can't Do
without You

❖ ❖ ❖

I have never heard or seen evidence of the Divine
Creator having created only one kind of anything—
from potatoes to people. The universe seems to love
abundance. As a storyteller, I like to try to shed a
little light on such mysteries. So years ago, I wrote
a story that began:

"Back then, in the beginning, God, obviously in
the ecstasy of creating Earth, was not thinking
about problems of overpopulation. It just didn't
dawn on him. He was just planning a species that
could fish, farm, take care of his property, and most
especially, that would have some general idea and
appreciation of the magnificence of what he was
trying to do. That is why he created man and
woman . . . So that he could get a population roll
going. It took a long time to get just a few mil-
lion people scattered around."

I am inspired by the tradition of the griot to offer
explanations and answers, no matter how big the
question might be or how subject to metamorpho-
sis. After all, every question has many answers. If
books grew on trees, there would be all kinds of

Bibles with varying testaments on how we all got started.

That nations sometimes behave as if the earth could accommodate only one kind of political and economic system—their own—strikes me as a foolhardy and dangerous proposition. Other systems must exist.

Our species thrives on oppositions. We couldn't walk or breathe without them.

I Miss the Russians

I miss the Russians as they used to be.
How dare the evil empire leap into the arms of
"One nation under God"—so fast.
Flatten Humanity's aspirations, dimensions
The nerve of the Union of Soviet Socialist
    Republics
To refuse to be the opposite pole—devil incarnate—
Enemy of overproduction, unemployment,
    recessions, depressions,
Deep and high crime and all other glories of
Global capitalism.

The cold war was a whirling dervish
A dizzying merry-go-round.
I don't know how we both didn't fall down
But the game was on. The lines were drawn
The stakes were high.
Didn't they realize that an unexpected stop like
Too sudden peace and
Everybody could almost die.

Couldn't somebody pull the Russian coattail?
"We can't do without you, bro.

Where you waz"
We need the U.S.S.RIANS to be the focal point—
    for war
And armament buildups
We'll look pretty silly flying, shooting, parading
All the latest hardware on various holidays and
Banging billions of bucks out of the budget
Just to keep some boots and some brass polished.

What about all the champeens of the world's
    underdogs
When they fight for justice
Better ways of life
What'll we call them?
Hell! Maybe soon to see one—let alone be one
We'll have to go to the zoo
"Mommie, Mommie, Mommie, take me to see a
    commie!"

Constitution, Bill of Rights
Noble aspirations—still
Can't they see? Don't they know?
The documents are in danger, need saving, bro!

The world needs oppositions—
A decent agitator class, man
To help keep some part of it honest, sister

To—like that main thing in the washing machine—
The righteous agitator—to get the dirt out!

Why couldn't you stay over on your side of the
     world.
Clean up the mess you made of a doctrine that—
Maybe wouldn't be too bad, if you could kick out
     the crooks—
Same as here. You just got lost somewhere.
But did you have to throw out the baby
With the bathwater?
Somebody's got to give socialism a chance
To get born and grow up.

Everybody on the same side of the ship—
Or trying to get there
Will sink the sucker.
You wasn't all bad, bro.
Who put up the first Sputnik
Who had the first man walk in space
Who started off glorifying working people!?

Tell you something. Bet you before long
You'll wish you'd stayed on your side of the
Human equation.
Stop thinking the grass on the football field is
Always really grass. Stop being jealous of the cousins
Who turned their noses up at you

When you were bleeding, sweating, overthrowing
Czars and royalty and exclusivities.
You had dreamed of embrace by
The thirteen colony's king-butt-kickers and the
Head harvesting revolutionaries of France.

You weren't all wrong.
You had a lot going for you.
You shoulda hung in there.
Made your commitment work.
Then maybe this Democracy business could
Someday, really do
The—of the—for the—by the—
With the—people thing.
History is sure happening, honey.

The Half-People

I am an export-import man, and my company's itinerary called for me to stop over in Nigeria on urgent business at the University of Ibadan. I hired a car at the airport in Lagos, the capital, and was soon on my way. The driver was Yoruba, an absolute authority on all things African, with plenty of questions about America and full of local wisdom and advice, especially for visitors. He talked; I didn't listen; it wasn't required. My mind was focused on the great writer I was on my way to meet, whose works were suddenly very much in demand back in America. I was planning my personally advantageous strategy to distribute them with a fair degree of ill-concealed excitement, which the driver may have mistaken for enthusiasm for his constant stream of information.

I must have dozed off, because when I woke up the car had turned off the highway and was pulling to a stop at a bicycle and auto repair shop in a tiny village square. It seemed a minor adjustment was needed that would take the approaching mechanic only a minute or so to make, and that then we would be on our way again. Meanwhile, the driver thought

I might be interested in seeing the site where a very important event in the history and traditions of the Yoruba people took place—the first battle of the Ajaye War. I complained to him that I was neither a tourist nor a historian, that my visit to this country was strictly business, and that if he couldn't get me to my destination in more of a hurry, I would have to look around for another car and driver. The size of his laughter, and a look around the tiny town square, including the "auto" repair shop, without seeing even a jackass in working condition made me understand at once that I was being ridiculous.

"I assure you, my brother, the vehicle will be ready soon—soon. Come let us wait in the shade. There is a very dear friend of mine I would like you to meet—a shopkeeper who is also my cousin."

The shop we entered was small, with neatly laid-out displays. A youngish man, wearing horn-rimmed glasses, carrying a book, and smiling warmly came forward to greet us.

"Femi Oladjula, please man, you must show some suitable African hospitality to this my friend from America, until I return."

Before I could protest, he was gone. I saw at a glance, almost in spite of myself, items of uncommon quality: intricately carved ivory, extraordinary beadwork, masks, statues, batiks, some paintings, fans, whisks, some beautifully tie-dyed cottons and silks for making *gheles*, highly favored by the women, and embroidered and brocaded *agbadas,* robes very popular with the men.

"Perhaps this piece here would also interest you." His long, bony finger indicated a figure carved of mahogany about 18 inches long, lying on an old velvet cushion a little apart from the other items on the counter. He picked it up so that I could get a better look. "An ancient object, found, it is said, at a local shrine. If you are interested—" Annoyance at my predicament almost made me shove the thing aside, but something odd, even chilling, about the statuette seized my attention. It was one half of a female figure that was carved to look as if it had been split in two from head to toe. Instead of two eyes there was just one. Instead of two ears, two arms, two hands, two legs, two feet, there was just one—all on the same side naturally.

"Where is the other half?" I demanded.

"There is no other half . . . this is all we know of how they looked . . ."

"Of how who looked?"

"Why the *Half-People*! They no longer exist, of course, but this is the only known carving of the last one of them ever seen. Would you like to buy it and take it to your country?"

"Half-People?. . ." I felt myself growing angry. "What do you take me for, a fool?"

"Trust me, my good friend, I speak the truth."

"Of course you do." I gave him back the thing and started outside. He firmly held me back.

"It is quite a story—I cannot tell you myself . . . but perhaps . . . since you are interested—"

I looked hard at the man and he stared at me, then slowly released his grip on my arm. In those seconds, images of people I'd seen with two necks, two heads, twelve fingers, three eyes, three arms, double rows of teeth bombarded my mind. Half people. How possible *is* the impossible? The man seemed earnest and honest. Can the matter be researched? Are there other proofs and artifacts? Can the main site be excavated? Did I dare hope this might prove to be a major discovery?

I felt a determination to have the thing well up in me. But I am a haggler, too skilled at negotiating to have let him know how very interested I was. "Interested? . . . In this thing?" I asked. "Something that's been split down the middle, with only one half left? A phony piece of work if ever I saw one, just meant for the foolish tourist you take me for."

The cousin reacted as if what I had said had hurt him beyond measure. With tears on the edge of his lower lids, he stretched out his arms and hung his head as if on a cross. Then slowly bringing his hands together as if to pray, he said, "Would you come this way, and please, watch your head."

I followed through a curtain of seeds, beads, and cowrie shells into a room so dark it suggested the void from which God made the world. A candle seemed to light itself. Sitting directly behind it, on a piece of goatskin was an earth-colored ancient-looking man with a full white beard. He wore a golden turban and a golden robe that was in obvious need of some repair. I was intrigued but suspicious. He snapped his head around and fixed me in a wild-eyed gaze.

"Why does the old man look at me like that. . . . Is he blind?"

"Yes. But only in one eye."

"Which eye is that?"

"No one has ever really known. I will speak to him. Perhaps I can persuade him to tell you the story."

"Tell me what story?"

"The story of the Half-People—who they were, where they came from, and how it came to be that they are no longer with us. There is a charge of course. . . ." He held out his hand.

I turned to leave, but there was something about the old man. Sitting there, he looked at the same time on the verge of flight. Half blind perhaps, yet

137

in the almost darkness I felt him see me wholly. Oh well! What else did I have to do while waiting for the driver to return except to listen. I reached into my pocket, took out a quarter, and put it into the cousin's outstretched hand. He looked embarrassed.

"He usually gets at least a dollar—one American dollar." I plucked the money from his hand and started out. Again he stopped me. "My cousin asked that I should be hospitable . . . I'll see what I can do." He took the quarter, crossed to the old man, kneeled, and held it out to him. The two of them talked in a language which I didn't understand. The old man sounded hurt then angry. The cousin sank lower and lower until he was almost prostrate. Finally he rose and came back to me. "Baba appreciates the fact that you are an American, but is this the best you can do? He usually gets at least a dollar—"

"I'll give him half." I got another quarter out of my pocket. "One half-dollar, and that's all!"

The old man, with a coin in each outstretched hand, slowly turned his head from one side to the other and suddenly screamed something with a staccato rhythm in the strange language. It was a startling moment.

I . . . tried to see into the holes that were his eyes to fathom which eye was blind—if indeed he were blind at all—when an eerie light emanated from both of them and held me transfixed until I was forced to drop my own eyes and lower my head. Then, in a soft, musical voice he began to unfold a strange story.

"How did the Half-People come to be? No one in history or science is quite sure. Some people say that once there lived a very accomplished tribe who ruled all the Earth. One day they went to their creator and said, 'We are so smart, we are so beautiful, so handsome, so superior in every way that you must make copies. You must make each of us two.' But the Maker, instead of making copies, split each one of them down the middle and said, 'Behold, now you are two!'

"After the Big Split, instead of two eyes they just had one, instead of two ears, two arms, two legs, they just had one—all on the same side, of course. Even their mouths were split right down the middle.

"What must life have been like in a time like this? Of course there were many things you could do with only a half self: You could comb your half head, rub your one eye, think your half-a-mind thoughts, scratch, pick your teeth, put food in your half mouth, and even sit down on your half-rump, if you were so disposed. Walking of course was impossible in the beginning. They had to hop to get from place to place. They couldn't cross their legs, or ride a camel. They could shake hands and snap fingers but they couldn't clap or applaud the one-armed jugglers. They could hit each other with the one fist they had, but they couldn't kick each other. Those who tried always fell flat on their half butts, and then had to wait until somebody came along to help them back onto their foot. Yes, things were quite a mess! For how on earth were they supposed to do the things they had done before the Big Split in order to survive? How to fish, farm, fight, finagle, fool around, and take care of their half babies became quite a challenge.

"After a time their leaders thought they had found a solution: The idea was simple enough: one half-person could strap himself—or herself—to another half-person, and in that way they could function like a whole person. They were so excited as they established Whole People Depots, Centers and bars where half-people came together in search of suitable other halves to help them make it through the rest of life.

"However, such arrangements were most often temporary, usually lasting no longer than a day. People quickly got tired of being hooked up with a stranger all the time. It was embarrassing. And also, unless you got to the supply places early there was no guarantee of making a good match. Most of the best halves would already be gone. Only all lefts, or all rights, might be left.

"At such times, matching would be especially difficult. Smokers might wind up with nonsmokers, a half-man with a half-woman, a slob with an effete, or a revolutionary with a reactionary, a pistol packer with a poet, or a manic with a depressive. Sometimes the other half might be too short, too thin, too mean, too slow, too fast, too talkative . . . too quiet, too bold, too old, too young, or have bad breath. Occasionally there would be a perfect match, except that the halves didn't speak the same language. It stands to reason that people could wind up pretty badly mismatched.

"Finally there was a total collapse. The frustrations became so enormous that it looked for a while as if the whole race of Half-People was doomed to extinction, that is, until one morning, when they all awoke to find that the new day for which so many of them had worked, and cried, and prayed— for which some of them had even died—had finally dawned. They were indeed on the threshold of peace, prosperity, and wholeness. There was a way, a simple, natural way for them to build a world where there would be no more Half-People, only whole people, healthy, singing people, sharing, caring people

. . . joyous, loving people worldwide, if only they would . . ."

And here the teller of the story stopped with his mouth wide open. Then he shook his head, closed his vacant eyes, and snapped his mouth shut. I, of course, protested, "What happened then? What was the secret? Did they become whole? How did they do it?" I knew if I knew those answers—no telling—I might become powerful—sought after. I might become rich. In my eagerness I leaped upon the old man and shook him, but he fell over in his seated position. He seemed to be in a deep trance. The cousin, speaking in the language, tried to wake the old man, but to no avail. He took me then by the arm and pushed me back through the beaded curtain into the shop.

"What's the matter with him?" I shouted. "Why has he stopped? I demand a refund."

"You gave him half-dollar, he told you half story."

"What!? . . . You mean, unless I give that old swindler another half-dollar, he won't tell me the rest of the story?"

"Well, if you could perhaps, make it a little more worth the old man's time, a dollar. Or maybe two . . . a small enough price I would think, then perhaps he would recover and I could persuade him to—"

"What does he take me for, a half-wit? No, no, not a cent more—" And with that I stormed out of the shop. I thought he might call me back. He did not. The car was waiting, I climbed in, and was soon on my way to Ibadan.

My business there took longer than I'd intended, three days and nights to be exact. And all the time I waited I grew more anxious. I must hear the rest of that story. It became almost an obsession. Finally, my business was completed. I had the driver speed me back to the small village, where we stopped in front of the shop of his cousin. I jumped out and ran inside.

"Where is he? . . . Where is the old man blind in one eye, who told me half a story? Where is he?"

"Oh, I am so sorry. He left three days ago."

"But the story, man, I must hear the rest of the story."

"I am sorry . . . I am so sorry. Of course, I would very much like to tell you myself, but—"

"But what?"

"It is not permitted. Only he is permitted—"

"Then where is he? Where is he? Which way did he go?"

"I doubt it very much that you can catch him, sir. If he has gone east, he is halfway to Enugu. If he has gone west, he is halfway to Benin. But since it is the rainy season, he is probably halfway north to Maiduguri."

"But the half-doll, the half statuette that was lying here on a pillow. Where is it, man, give it to me. Name your own price, but please, at least let me have the thing."

"He took that, too. I am sorry, sir, so sorry . . ."

I went back home to the U.S. and busied myself with my work, but I could not forget.

Many nights I hear the old man, I see him, but when I reach out to grab him, to demand that he tell me the rest of the story, I wake, and he's gone. How I wish I could call back time. I'd give the old man whatever money he might ask. The habit of the haggle, however—about another's worth, with respect to their goods, their services, their gifts or their person—is hard to overcome. But I would pay him much more than a dollar. That's why you see me now, packed and ready to travel back to Nigeria, back to find that same car, the same driver, with his same cousin. God help me, but I must know the end, the other half of the story! I must, because here I am before you, half out of my mind. Did the

Half-People become whole? How? How? I must know. I must! I must! Do you know? Can you tell me the end of the story? Did the Half-People become whole? How? How? I must know! I must! I must! Do you know? Can you—please! Please . . . tell me the end of the story!

Isn't Life Peculiar?

❖ ❖ ❖

Many of my favorite sayings are about time.

"Procrastination is the thief of time."
"Time waits for no man (or woman)."
"The road to hell is paved with good intentions."
"Time flies as if it's in a hurry to escape and be done with humanity."
"Time in its madness scatters dust to blind us."

In short, time hasn't got all day.

Dream the dreams. Force the issues fast. Make your prints in the sands of time before the next wave washes over or the sea demons cut off your foot. We have to keep on hopping. This is the way of knowledge and pain. It's almost unbearable. Not a single second can we call back, reexamine, or do over again. Where does time go when it's gone? Just recycled, perhaps.

Life *is* an incomparably fascinating play, and I'd like to stay around for the third act. As the character Gitlow says in Ossie's play, *Purlie Victorious,* when reading about the Civil War in a comic book, "This sure is a good story. I wonder how it's gon' come out?" I wonder about crossing over that

149

final bridge, death. There will probably be some giggles and gasps, lots of silent, solemn, surprising revelations—and answers to questions I've been asking for a long, long time.

I hope time will have something like a face, a substance that I can run my fingers over, and a hand that I can shake.

Time To

When I was sixteen
I picked up everywhere I could find them,
Seconds, minutes, hours, days, weeks, months,
    years
TIME—my time
My very own time
All mine time
And put that heavy load in a plastic bag
Tied it with a wire
Put it under bolt and electronic key
In the deep deep freeze
At Chase Manhattan
(The home of my main friend.)
I said
I'll draw it out when I decide to live
But *now*—right *now*
I'm gon' sneak through the no-time spaces
And get myself together.

I know the world is shot
Gone to pot, but
Maybe I'll make new rules
Soon as I start my time.

People crying dying
Busy dying deaths
But that don't bother me
I got no time for funerals and
Bomb-bullet wounds and babies and
Hospitals and hunger
And leftovers laying in the street
Later for all that
Take care of all that
Later.
Right now, honey, I'm just vamping 'til ready.

Now, how—what is this sliding in on me
Through the walls and patting my cheeks
With stone cold, bony fingers
At this crack of dawn.
Look here, you cold gray man
You lost your mind?
Back off!
You trying to stop me
Can't you see I'm getting dressed
On my way to draw my time—
My minutes, hours, and so forth—
Here's my stopped-clock passbook
See these deposits drawing interest?
My life so far is a holding action
A marking time

A doing nothing special
A taking no chances
A straddling the fence
A ducking and puffing
A making no waves
Why, I'm just sixteen
Won't be seventeen
'Til I decide to draw out another year.

Get your bony fingers offa my flesh!
What you mean
You dried up thing
That you got me down for sixty years old.
Man, you crazy—Let go!
Come on with me
Let me show you something
Now this here is Chase Manny
My friend
And he's gonna take us to the vault.
Where is it?
Where's my time?
Whoa, hold it, hey wait now
Don't be pulling on me
I didn't live, laugh, and love yet
Didn't give, care, and cry yet
I didn't learn and create and
Turn the world upside down yet.

Gone!
Don't tell me it's gone.
All, all, all my precious time
Gone . . .
Gone . . .
All *my* time gone!
My time . . .
Where is my time?!

Daughter

When I was young I would
Study my mother sometimes to try to
Imagine that she really knew or was
Capable of appreciating the love of a man—
The too warm feelings in a warm bed
Let alone if she could remember ecstasies.

Despite the presence of my affectionate father.
I made up my mind that she did not remember
That her thoughts were all of me and my
    fulfillments.
That she didn't belong to the club where
    temptations and desires
Collected heavy dues.

I thought of her as almost saint
A creature innocent of fleshly feelings
And jealousies and lusts.
Pedestal material. Respectable.
To be respected and adored
To be counted on when I needed example
Comfort and understanding and money.

From time to time though
Watery images wiggle through my mind and
I think I remember still—as a child—
Mama screaming through a locked door
Bathroom door, it was.
Screaming. And pounding fists and tears
And all the damns and got-damns. And
Daddy talking loud and finally
Coming in or coming out to grab her
    wrists and still the flailing fist.
And she still crying and the two of them
    hugging and
Watching Daddy pick Mama up and carry her—
    as long ago she carried me—off to bed.

As I look down now at
Hands folded across each other in gloved stillness
Full lips pressed thin and painted pale
By a would-be Rembrandt rectifying the sensuous
For the death position
I deny such images with a finality.
No.   No.   There were never any screams.
There were no wild sweaty clutchings
No nail diggings making bloody my father's flesh.
No receiving of deep rhythmic probes
Bursting into ecstasies, other dimensions.
Unlike all-embracing air, passion should
    come with some measure of exclusivity.

Even to "have at it" like so-called lesser animals
Should surely be a privilege.
Accidental, occasional, seasonal if ever
    for our mothers
Our fathers, our teachers, our leaders,
Should be reserved for youth. Because
We need examples. People to look up to.
Immediate saints to assure us that fires
Don't necessarily have to rage.
That they can be steady, glowing embers,
Issuing just sufficient warmths that
Slip quietly, beautifully into ashes.
The world needs living ashes
To soothe, to calm, to annoint, to cover, to
Make alkaline the acids and to
Cool out the raging fires.
My own tongue is swollen
Too much used and abused
I myself am too busy with business,
    bruises and bread
Covered with kisses and longings.

Oh, why can't I have—
Mother, leave me your virtues. I need
Collateral to ride to heaven on.
I need you to see me through
To my salvation.

The Dream Droppers

The dream you see is a demanding, hard-trick
    mistress.
Whenever one short circuits the alarm system
Some late night or early morning and
Invades my space—I just want to shout—
Oh, for heaven's sake go someplace else!
Wreck complacency in some other head.
What is it you dream droppers would try to have
    me do?
How long an anguish is this job?
How many headlines announcing defeat of yet
Another dream
Before you realize—I'm not the one to drag dreams
    to light
Dry them off, give them feet and voice.

Don't you dream droppers realize how many brains
    you've
Caused to be exploded?
Bodies dropped from airplanes
Necks stretched, flesh shredded
How many skeletons spined with principle
To crumble to dust in jail?

I've laid my stuff on the line for the last time,
Dream droppers.
Finally out on bail, got a reality job now.
Mortgage.
Looking for some peace of mind

But the dreams come anyway and
I drop them like goody gum drops
Into the waiting minds of those who have loved me
And go about my business.

From time to time though
I sneak a peak around a corner
To see if one of those explosive, ethereal
Dangerous aspirations
Takes hold, stays alive. Grows.
Because every now and then
A dream does put on flesh, stands tall
And walks!
A dream does happen every once in a while, you
    know.

The Pain Taker

The ad in the *New York Amsterdam News* specifically stated: *"Wanted: Pain Taker.* To take all pain." Of course, payment was not at issue. Your best pain takers want to assume as much pain as possible and not shed a tear. The payment is the pain. Another preferred attribute of a really desirable pain-plucker is that he or she or he-she or she-he be black, meaning BUL-LACK—pure, if possible. That's why I chose to place my ad in this Harlem-located, black-oriented publication. Anyway, and to make a long story short, by the time the eighth applicant showed up in my debt-ridden abode, I was getting slightly nervous. There were some likely prospects—but none that you'd call unconditional, e.g., one did not pain take on Sundays; one couldn't stand confusion (only one pain at a time); one didn't do blood, and so forth. Then through the walls, here slides something or someone, cringing, crawling, almost invisible and seeming to need a pain fix real bad. At first I thought it was a woman; then, when the figure finally fell into full focus, I could see it was a he. And UGLY! I thought I knew about ugly, because I'm ugly myself, but this was a hurting ugly, just to look at, let alone be. Doubt crept in. How much multiple pain would it take to make a dent in what a pain taker this bent-up-looking needed? Did I have enough? Well, my first name is Trouble. Also my middle two and last two names. (Troubled Fifth, my friends call me.) I figured I could make it. I decided on Dothan.

Now I'm not going into all my troubles. That's what I got Dothan for. But on my job, promotion after promotion all around me, and never me. Then I got fired. My wife left me. My two boys quit speaking to me; and my side hustle was put down by some mad Mediterraneans who threatened to end all my pains with no couth. But when I began seeing my self-substance leaving me and floating around in the air like feathers from a busted pillow, I knew I was in trouble. There I was drifting by, bit by bit; and no matter how hard I tried to catch and stuff myself back through ears, mouth, nose, the top of my head, I just kept leaving. That's when I began to really worry; and, as I said, that's when I put that ad in the paper and got my pain taker, Dothan.

Dothan went everywhere with me. Everything began picking up. No money for the rent, Dothan maneuvers and the landlord gives me a receipt: "Rent. Paid In Full Forever." Somebody insults me, Dothan lands a whammy and the cousin drops.

Never will forget the time when I was cool, trying to make a gainful move and a car slows down, a little glint of steel muzzle—bang! Dothan sticks his hand over my heart and catches the bullet.

This day, however, I was sitting in the middle of the floor waiting for Dothan to go with me to see about a really important undercover undertaking and the little pain taker doesn't show. With my head down, I'm thinking maybe somebody stole him from me. Who wouldn't want a PT like Dothan. I've got to speak to him, though, about the pain of waiting—even for the pain taker. Then I look up and WOW! Dothan is just standing there—no knock, no cheery "Good morning—it's going to be a great day for you"—no nothing. Just standing there with his legs pressed together like he's got to go to the bathroom, arms twisted around his body like he's trying to hold himself together, eyes frogged out and shiny. Then it begins to happen. Two big sloppy tears fell, then four, then six until his whole little body was shaking and drenched with tears. When he reached to wipe his left eye, all his insides fell out. Blood was everywhere. I couldn't believe it—Dothan honking, bleeding like that and dumping *his* troubles in *my* living room. I told him to shut up, get himself together or leave!

"For Pete's sake—what's the matter? You are reneging on our agreement!" Then he told me between sobs what happened.

"I can take the pain of birth, the pain of battle, diseases, disappointment, of poverty, insanity, insomnia, injustice, indifference, of envy, greed, hopelessness, helplessness, loneliness, obesity, discrimination, and death—to name a few. But there is just one pain I cannot take: *Unhappy!* You are still not *happy*; and my boss, The Great Pain Taker, has fired me! Snatched me off the job because I didn't make you sing, laugh, dance for joy. D-d-didn't make you—d-d-didn't make you—HAPPEE!"

"Happy! What's happy?" I was shocked. "Yeah, you brought me a little luck, but just keeping up with it makes me mean, nervous, suspicious, and needing a whole lot more."

"But it is written. By now, you are supposed to he happy." I could see he was getting mad. "You have ruined my reputation. You have shattered my ugly depth and thrown my metabolic pain absorber permanently out of gear." He began to jump up and down screaming, "You are not Hap-p-e-e-e! You are not Hap-p-e-e-e!—" until he became a blur.

Then I started jumping up and down screaming. "That's not fair! Not fair. *Now* who will I get to take my life's crap? Console me, understand me, give me everything I want and love me love me love me. Not fair! Not fair! Liar!" But Dothan had disappeared, insides, blood, and all.

Well, who needs him. Who needs a pain-taking liar. Dothan lied. He is not unconditional. I yelled after him anyway.

"Happy. Humph! Your boss can read, can't he? He seen the headlines lately? This world is rough! It takes a miracle just to keep on breathing. It ain't no soap opera out here. Ma-a-an—this is life!"

Today Is Ours

It seems easier to sell papers, commercials, or tickets if you focus on sorrow, disappointment, and pain. How about emphasizing the good, the beautiful, and the joyous for a change? If that approach does not make money for anyone, at least it will be blessed proof of our sanity. I welcome any sign these days that people have managed to keep at least one good nerve intact.

Someday . . .
    I want to write a book about all
    The caring people,
    And to send up prayers of thanksgiving
    And do dances of joy.

There's evidence everywhere you look that life is good. Just look at a double Dutch jump rope marathon. I've always been fascinated by this incredible game. It ought to be part of the Olympics. Legs, braids flying, intense faces, arms attached to ropes turning, turning in the air. Sudden dancing. One girl, two girls in and out create a whirlwind of motion that I could watch for hours. Hearts, minds, and bodies in exclamation point precision. How could any team be better than this one, right now? But better teams do come. When I see the despair on the shining, brown faces of girls who missed a step or tangled a rope, I want to shout, "Hey, little girl! It's okay. You'll win later or another day!"

The actor Beah Richards's grandmother used to recite this anonymous poem. For years it's been my signature anthem:

> Today is ours; let's live it.
> And love is strong; let's give it.
> A song can help; let's sing it.
> And peace is dear; let's bring it.
> The past is gone; don't rue it.
> Our work is here; let's do it.
> The world is wrong; let's right it.
> The battle is hard; let's fight it.
> The road is rough; let's clear it.
> The future vast; don't fear it.
> Is faith asleep; let's wake it.
> Today is ours; let's take it!

My One Good Nerve

The nerves once functioned like a symphony
But the struggle got rough
Promises, fulfillments, didn't match
All the overlooking, overcoming got too tough.
Vipping when I needed to vop.
Going straight ahead when I needed to stop.
Spending life's blood in gambling joints
Cashing in my gold for chips
To plunk down on irrelevancies, stupidities
And detours past too many main points.
Forgetting to cool out the noises
Pay attention
Living life ad lib, ad hoc, at random.

People, events, descriptions, definitions like
Tiny jumbled jigsaw puzzle pieces
Screaming to get ordered
Fitted into a serene and beautiful picture
Of me making sense
But the madnesses, contradictions,
Procrastinations, absurdities took over
So hysteria just torpedoed the territory
Stripped all the nerves
Except one.

So I'm standing here outside
The last gate to myself
With my fist balled up and dug in my hips
Gonna put on my glasses
And poke out my lips
Ready to do battle
Hook a mean curve
Before I let anything get on
My one good nerve.

Then together and focused
I will stroll on through
To the power and glory
With a glass of water on my head
Then hold for a gentle pat on my back
As I present myself
With my one good nerve
Intact.

Time. Time.

This is my time
This is your time
This our time together
Time—Time
Creeping out from the rocks of ages
The seas, sun, moon, rain, green leaves
From nothing
From everything that ever was
From microbe time to
Flesh and bones and blood time
Countless invisible tentacles
Making me distinct, separate
And just like you and
Especially like you
Your face a privilege
Your touch a recording
Your deaths all mine
In glory or despair
Part of the pattern—the dizzying pattern
That keeps on trying to improve itself
Throughout your—my time
Time—the traveler—snatching
Snatching at forever—searching

Searching for the unraveler
That perfects the pattern.
Mean time
To laugh, to give, to cry
And try, try, try to
Reach out on this special ride.
To shout—shout
I want to love you—you
You—I love you
This is the trip
This is my time.
This is your time your
Time is my time. Our
Time together time time
The always today time time
The always now time
That gives eternity its dimension
That sparks everlasting's come
Come and find me come
Come and take me fire.

Double Dutch

Oh-oh girl—
You broke your stride
Did that put
A dent in your pride?
That's alright my little friend
Don't get mad.
Don't jump bad.
Reassess your situation
Make another evaluation
Then
Take a deep breath
Say a little prayer
And jump right on back in there.

Calling All Women

Calling all sisters. Calling all
Righteous sisters.
Calling all women. To steal away
To our secret place. Have a meeting
Face to face. Look at the facts
And determine our pace. Calling all
Women.

We want to reach—first and second
And
Third world women
Come together!
Women in and outside the power structure—
Working women,
Welfare women,
Women who feel alienated and isolated
Women who are all frustrated
Who have given up—women—women
Questioning women—women
Unpolarized and unorganized.
Ostracized. Tired of being penalized
Come help us start to bridge the gaps

Racial, cultural, or generation
We want action and veneration.

These men, these men they
Just ain't doing it.
They've had hundreds of years
Now they 'bout to ruin it.

Kitchen, office, ex-prison women
Singing, dancing, diapering women
Old and young and middle-aged women
Make this scene
Oh yes, and bring your lunch!

Problems, problems, common problems
That we make and cause each other
Sister, daughter, old grandmother
Female child you can bring your little brother
Take the subway, grab a cab
Saddle your mule
Bike it, limo
Take a choo-choo, fly
Or pick 'em up and lay 'em down.

Socialism, capitalism, communism
Feminism, womanism, lesbianism

Here-and-now or futurism
We just can't afford a schism
We got to get together or die.

Now is the time for an evolution
Let's all search and find solution
For how we'll make that next revolution
Or die.
Oh yes. And don't forget your lunch!

Afterword

I have been working the words as an actor on stage, television, and in films for many years. I started writing when I was about nine years old. My mother's heartbeat quickened. She sent one of the first poems I had written to the New York *Amsterdam News,* and they published it:

> The graveyard is so quiet and lonely
> A place for dead people only
> Too late to live
> When all they had to give
> Is laid beneath the sod.

She preserved this great work in a scrapbook that I have to this day.

About thirty years later, I began again to string words together into thoughts of sorts and to call myself a writer.

Thank God for the life expectancy increase. I'm praying that if I be a real nice ol' lady, the Big Daddy of All will put me on the longevity track and serve me up a Reely Big Break as an actor as well as a writer.

I don't want to sound like an earthly ingrate. I've received much recognition, many awards and degrees, and general approbation. I belong to a marvelous sorority, Delta Sigma Theta, and a couple of Halls of Fame. And I'm in the process of picking a horse—Baptist, Methodist, Unitarian, or another—for a presumed gallop to glory.

The point is: Now that I'm only in the kindergarten of Ancient, I think I've finally found the confidence to work the words the way I want to, to present myself and other authors and their ideas in the distinct pitches and rhythms that are too often overlooked. Longevity makes sense.

We need to keep talking to each other from heart to heart, facing ideas and probabilities that emanate from spirit. One-on-one, face-to-face expressions will enhance our importance to each other in profound ways and lead to a greater commitment to love, warm embraces, fireplaces, and watching waves wash the shore.